PLEASANT THE SCHOLAR'S LIFE:
IRISH INTELLECTUALS AND THE CONSTRUCTION OF THE NATION STATE

MAURICE GOLDRING is France's leading historian of Irish culture. The French translator of a number of Sean O'Casey's plays, he contributes to publications ranging from *Le Monde Diplomatique* to *Fortnight* and the *Irish Literary Supplement*. Maurice Goldring is Professor of Irish Studies at the University of Paris; his books include *Belfast: From Loyalty to Rebellion*, *Le Drame de l'Irlande* and *La République Populaire de France*.

Pleasant the Scholar's Life:

Irish Intellectuals and the Construction of the Nation State

Maurice Goldring

Serif

London

First published 1993 by
Serif
47 Strahan Road London E3 5DA

British Library Cataloguing-in-Publication Data.
A catalogue record for this book
is available from the British Library.

ISBN 1 897959 06 0

Photoset in North Wales by
Derek Doyle and Associates, Mold, Clwyd
Printed and bound in Great Britain by
Biddles of Guildford

For Laurent, Sophie and Robin,
in their order of appearance

Contents

Foreword

Chapter 1 and parts of Chapter 2 and Chapter 3 of this book are heavily revised versions of *Faith of Our Fathers*, published in Dublin in 1982. Much of the new material was earlier published in different forms in the following journals: *Etudes irlandaises, Irlande politique et sociale, Making Sense, Fortnight, Encrages, Trema, Saothar* and *Les Langues modernes.* The French version of *Faith of Our Fathers* was published in 1976 as *Irlande: Idéologie d'une révolution nationale*. The book was well received in both France and Ireland at the time. I was then a Marxist and a member of the French Communist Party, and Marxism was the method by which I sought to reveal the class interests lurking behind the mask of cultural nationalism. I am no longer a Communist and have abandoned large chunks of what I considered then to be part and parcel of Marxism. I have since added to my preoccupations the notion of gender, as masculine power seems to me to be an under-appreciated aspect of Irish nationalism and, indeed, of nationalism more generally. By the same token, power conflicts pertain not only to class but also to questions of caste and ethnicity. But these new preoccupations have not altogether obliterated the Marxist approach, which to my mind has not lost its power as a means of investigating social movements. My interest shifted from nationalism to the class struggle and then from the class struggle back to nationalism, and I have tried to understand how national identities can be channels for class interests. A nationalist demonstration in Dublin or Belfast does not lose its class character simply because it proclaims itself a nationalist gathering, just as a strike or trade union rally in either city cannot fail to have a certain connection with 'the national question'.

Another important aspect of my evolution over almost two decades is connected with the crisis of Communist forms of organisation inherited from Leninism. The notion of 'vanguardism' is inherently warlike, and I recognised in the self-definition of Dublin intellectuals as well as in the violence of the paramilitaries the idea of a self-selecting elite which thinks it knows what is best for the people. Thunderous excommunications, whether in republican ranks or cultural circles, share the same logic as Communist parties, with the resulting danger of a totalitarian state. Democracy, on the other hand, must first learn to recognise that different ideas must be understood, tolerated and maybe even considered as not necessarily wrong.

I wish to thank my intellectual companions in this venture. My acknowledgements go to the late Professors Frechet and Rafroidi, who supervised my first attempts at trying to understand Irish nationalism; to François Poirier and Paul Brennan, organisers of research groups in which much of this work has been presented and discussed; Martine Spensky, who introduced me to gender studies and has helped me more than she is aware; Professor René Gallissot, who has made important contributions to the study of nationalism; my Irish colleagues and friends Paul Bew, who read the manuscript and contributed valuable comments, and David Harkness and John Darby; Stephen Hayward, publisher, editor and friend, has as usual been demanding, helpful and encouraging. Thanks also to the Institute of Irish Studies (Queen's University, Belfast), the Centre for Comparative Studies of Social Movements (CIMOS, University of Paris VIII), the British Council and the CNRS, all of which institutions contributed to making my work possible.

Introduction

A mass movement becomes political when it embraces intellectuals, that is to say men and women who have acquired, through a long training at university or elsewhere, know-how and knowledge that enable them to give theoretical coherence to a social movement, to understand the complexity of the present or to dream about the future. Their active commitment to the movement is the surest sign which distinguishes a revolution from a revolt. Gavroche, in *Les Misérables*, could sing, '*C'est la faute à Voltaire, c'est la faute à Rousseau*' – Voltaire is to blame, Rousseau is to blame. One could add that Locke, Thomas Paine, Marx and Lenin are all to blame, but no future Gavroche will ever sing, '*C'est la faute à Charlie Haughey, c'est la faute à Gerry Adams, c'est la faute à Ian Paisley*.'

Let us look briefly at the definition of 'intellectuals' given above. By 'intellectuals' we should not limit ourselves to academics, ideologues or writers; intellectuals can be poets or economists, civil engineers or priests, army officers or primary-school teachers. It is the presence of intellectuals which distinguishes a peasant outburst from a social revolution, and in nineteenth-century rural societies those intellectuals could be officers or priests, students or teachers. The riots in the black ghettos in the United States ceased to be seen as disorderly outbreaks when the movement embraced students, preachers, writers, film-makers, historians and others who were able to rake through the past and evaluate the present, giving back a collective memory to the black community and projecting its experience into the future.

Many in the West adopted a superior smile when they saw on their television screens pictures of Iran being stormed by surging crowds led by their religious intellectuals. The whole spectacle looked so medieval, like a poor man's crusade, Western observers said dismissively. In fact, the presence of mullahs and imams meant that the Iranian revolution had to be taken seriously; this was not a riotous outburst but an important social movement, and control of the state itself was at stake. In South Africa violent demonstrations did not at first really frighten the wardens of apartheid: a few well-trained riot police could overcome the young protesters in no time at all. An angry outburst has no future. What shook white South African society to its roots was the presence of writers, poets, priests and others through whom the movement had acquired a political project, an image of the future, that could no longer be beaten into the ground with tear-gas, batons and guns.

The values created or repeated by the literary revival at the end of the nineteenth and beginning of the twentieth century filtered down through Irish society as a whole. For Augustine Birrell, Chief Secretary for Ireland, literature and drama of the time were 'of far more real significance than the monthly reports of the Royal Irish Constabulary', and for the historian Roy Foster, reflecting on Birrell's remark, literature was another aspect of a maturing society.[1]

The role played by intellectuals is particularly important in rural societies. A peasant nation seldom finds its representatives within itself; its ideas, demands and aspirations go through channels and leaders external to it, firstly, at local level, through village priests, or perhaps the primary-school teacher, then, at a higher level, through the urban middle class.[2] The relationship between intellectuals and mass struggles, between the cultural avant-garde and mass movements, is ever present in Irish nationalism. The tension which was thus revealed has never really ceased. The intellectuals tried to get on with their own work while the movement demanded that they commit themselves to the cause. It was these very conflicts and tensions which were proof of the movement's strength. It is worth mentioning that in contemporary Ireland, especially the North, the major political movements, both nationalist and loyalist, do not have intellectuals, as I have used the term, in their ranks. There is a great deal of propaganda but no intellectual creation that is rooted in the political struggle. The North's many talented playwrights, poets and novelists want no part in the conflict, even if it sometimes forms the background to their work. This absence of intellectuals from the contemporary 'Troubles' is a useful index for gauging the historical weight and limits of those upheavals.

The interest and importance of Ireland in the study of the relations between intellectuals and 'the people' lies in the respective fascination of political leaders for poets and of poets for political leaders. They emulated each other in eloquence and competed for power or influence over the people. The writers wanted to be leaders or prophets, and their models were O'Connell and Parnell, while political leaders wanted to be remembered in the same way as the bards. Yeats without poetical genius becomes de Valera. All were ready to stamp the wax before it hardened. De Valera believed that:

> The Irish genius has always stressed spiritual values and intellectual rather than material values. That is the characteristic that fits the Irish people in a special manner for the task ... of helping to save western civilisation.[3]

Yeats thought it a good thing that Ireland was not rich, holding that it is always poor nations which achieve great things in art. The Irish people had not been corrupted by commercialism and so formed an audience endowed with qualities of imagination capable of appreciating serious drama.[4]

It is common sense to assume that the cultural renaissance took root in the ruins of political leadership after the fall of Parnell, but it could also be construed as a sign that the political aspiration for national independence was growing. The years from 1890 to 1920 were not peaceful ones. Land agitation did not cease, and after the Wyndham Acts the peasantry was flexing the muscles of its new-found economic power. Labour unrest was also a permanent feature on the political landscape, North and South, culminating in the great Belfast strikes of 1907 and 1911 and the Dublin strike and lock-out in 1913. The question of who would rule the new country was becoming more acute. In the late 1960s, I had the privilege of attending a conversation between the late Sean McEntee, then the last survivor of the 1916 Rising, and Conor Cruise O'Brien. Conor Cruise O'Brien, as is his wont, provoked McEntee with a sweeping statement: '1916 was a mistake,' he declared. Sean McEntee replied, 'Maybe it was, but I'm glad I was part of it.' McEntee's daughter Maureen added, with superb clear-sightedness, 'Conor, your grandfather was a member of the Irish Parliamentary Party. You were part of the elite. My father was the son of a publican. He would never have become minister without 1916. We would not have a fine house, his children would never have been to the best schools.' Ruefully, Conor Cruise O'Brien answered, 'Exactly, your people pushed mine aside.' This process was exactly summed up in Sean O'Faolain's phrase 'the putsch of the middle classes'.

After the elections of 23 November 1918, Sinn Fein became the leading political force in Ireland. It was this group of elected deputies who were to lead the struggle for independence in the future. The Sinn Fein deputies comprised nine journalists, seven teachers, eighteen members of the commercial professions, of whom ten were small shop-keepers and one wholesaler, five representatives of nationalist organisations, two municipal workers and two legal clerks.[6] White-collar workers, the professions and small traders were, therefore, all represented, but the developing upper-middle class, the working class and the peasantry who made up the majority of the country were not represented in Dail Eireann. There were a few token women. The poets had also disappeared; they were useful for being shot, not for taking the lead in serious matters.

In the growing confrontation with Great Britain, the working class, upper-middle class and the peasantry all had particularly strong claims on the leadership of the struggle for independence, but none of these social groups had sufficient cohesion to take over the leadership. Important demands of the peasantry had been met, and as new landowners they had become more cautious. The working class had been weakened after the 1913 lock-out and was divided from its northern counterpart in Belfast. The upper-middle class in Ireland was young and was also divided between North and South. As we shall see, its attitude during the 1913 conflict in Dublin, in spite of an apparent victory, had also weakened it politically.

In order to rule a country, a group must have an ambition, an image of the future acceptable to a wide range of people. The goal of the leading groups in the working class could be summed up in one word – socialism – which was certainly not acceptable to the majority of the population. The most powerful industrialists lived in Belfast and their ambition was to maintain, indeed to strengthen, the link with Britain and the Empire and they could not aspire to take over the nation's leadership.

> In the ranks of the Irish party today not one single man can claim to actively represent the interests of banking or industry in the country. How has this change come about? What is the explanation for this total divorce between the financial and industrial interests in the country and its parliamentary representatives?[7]

The middle classes, urban and rural, were therefore left holding the field, traders, small manufacturers and the professions in the towns, civil servants, primary-school teachers and priests in the countryside. This situation was the result of Ireland's historical evolution during the nineteenth century. Following the Act of Union, Dublin had lost its position as a capital city. The professional prospects offered by a capital were closed off; administrative and judicial careers were severely limited. Teaching was a poor second due to the low level of schools and universities. While both the upper-middle and working classes could and did develop, the middle class described above formed

> a small hard stratum of discontented men possessed with pride, ambition, and ability, but with no prospects and no cause to love England. These lawyers, doctors, journalists, teachers, poets, engineers, clerks, recusant pastors and other professional men of the middle class made a permanent knot of leaders for Irish nationalism.[8]

This social group, of somewhat mixed origins, was adaptable enough to absorb aspirations which were sometimes at odds with one another. The cultural revival movement was able to provide it with a number of possible models. It was a pool of ideals, a mixum-gatherum of mythologies into which all could dip according to their personal aspirations. Ernie O'Malley, for example, was a shoneen, aping the manners and fashions of the English;[9] fortunately, however, his nurse told him the stories and legends of ancient Ireland, the tale of mighty Fionn, the epic of Cuchulain, which was sufficient to turn him into enough of an Irishman to be laughed at in Dublin schools and to fight with his school-mates about the respective merits of Cuchulain and Buffalo Bill.[10] After 1916, Dublin became a hotbed of patriotism, nationalist songs were sung and whistled in the streets, poems by Pearse, MacDonagh and Plunkett were reprinted. O'Malley 'reconstructed their work and their ideals' as Ireland became an obsession for him.[11]

Literary clubs and cultural organisations became so many recruiting agents for the volunteers. Money collected after traditional musical events was used to buy arms. Rooms used for evening lectures became drill halls in daytime and cultural enthusiasm was a prerequisite for military enthusiasm, not an aim in itself. 'The men had little use for anyone who was not a believer in physical force. Gaelic Leaguers and members of the Sinn Fein Clubs who did not belong to the Volunteers were sneered at.'[12]

When Southern Ireland became independent, the conflicts and policies all had to be dipped into the magic fountain of cultural nationalism. No one exploited this more than de Valera. For him, independence had a price: 'I know that certain costs will go up but that is necessary. You cannot have omelettes and not break eggs.'[13] Dev compared the Irish people to a servant who decides to live in a cottage rather than in the luxury of serfdom;[14] as a Christian country, Ireland's resistance to oppression has been spiritual, religious and linguistic so that in times of hardship, people are 'satisfied with frugal comfort' because they dream of a future of cosy homesteads, sturdy children, athletic youths, comely maidens and firesides as forums for the wisdom of serene old age.[15]

Popular political movements of various political complexions have generally followed the same pattern since the beginning of the twentieth century. They came to power after a long period of people's mobilisation and subsequently their leaders had to come to grips with hard reality. Control of the state secures political power but does not guarantee a friendly international environment or a healthy economy. Governments have to take difficult decisions and those decisions tend to be accompanied by a sharp drop in their supporters' fighting spirit. The dream of a Gaelic Ireland has been used *ad nauseam* to fill the vacuum and revive popular enthusiasm. Everybody knows what is left of the dream, but it worked and, perhaps because it is the only one available, it even works today.

Franco Venturi, studying nineteenth-century Russian populism, showed how that movement could degenerate into conservative, reactionary and nationalistic rhetoric while at the same time being a positive response to the feeling of inferiority towards the West:

> An idea which seems to be looking backward, which apparently refers to the past, which seems to prefer what has been and excludes what will be – is such an idea in itself and because of itself condemned to play a negative role? Does it not rather represent a case of *reculer pour mieux sauter*, an attempt which could be fruitful in so far as it preserves what was precious from the past so as to be able to pass it on in the future?[16]

The competing images came, via Belfast, from Britain, celebrating shipyards and factories, industrial and material success. The working-class movement, torn asunder by conflicting loyalties to green, Gaelic Ireland and to black, industrial Ireland, has produced grey policies.

Ireland was threatened by stronger neighbours and stronger cultures; the country's new leaders were self-conscious – they had to justify their power to their people, to the world, and maybe first of all to themselves. Irish political mythology should not be studied as a political platform but above all as a voice, a conscience, giving dignity and assurance to the new political elite. The shopkeepers, lawyers and teachers needed a strong moral incentive and cohesion in order to push Conor Cruise O'Brien's people aside. It was all there, in the cultural programmes, popular novels, songs and poems. The only real losers were those writers who thought their speeches would be taken seriously.

Urban Intellectuals

In late nineteenth-century Ireland, writers of all sorts – journalists, poets, novelists and playwrights – came forward to put their stamp, that is to say their word, on the nation. There was a kind of goldrush towards a true national culture. Like Yeats, they considered themselves to be guides, prophets and Messiahs – flaming torches of the spirit. 'How one might seal with the right image the soft wax before it began to harden?' Yeats wondered.[17] They carried precedents in their heads – they felt themselves carried forward by the nation's history.

To justify the cultural role they had taken on they were able to choose from a multitude of cultural models. The poet's role in Gaelic society inspired them. Wolfe Tone, Robert Emmet and Thomas Davis had all placed great emphasis on the value of words. In the rhetoric of the Fenian leaders, the expression 'Give the word' invested language with a sacred character.

Intellectuals had to work hard to secure their place in the front line of the struggle, however, and met with considerable resistance. Too many things about them turned them into strangers, and they were looked on suspiciously by most members of the population. Their careers and fame had often been made in England. Their writing was still addressed to the educated audience of the country which had trained them. Nationalists wondered whether these people had not come looking for patents of nobility of another type and whether cultural colonialism was looting the riches of the country to give new lease of life to a 'foreign' literature. Nationalist struggles had led writers away from England and Europe and now they found themselves foreigners in their own land.

In spite of those difficulties, no one could escape the imagery of modern Ireland they had created. Of course, the tendency of those who in the final analysis give an account of events is to exaggerate their own personal or collective influence. The degree of pride expressed by W.B. Yeats when he wondered if the words he had written had sent men to be killed by the English is almost inconceivable. But Yeats placed himself in a firmly established tradition, and half a century earlier the *Nation* was publishing poems extolling the irresistible power of the Voice and the Pen:

And the world will say, 'No power can stay
The Voice and the fearless Pen!'
Hurrah!
Hurrah! for the Voice and Pen![18]

Reading some accounts of this period, one sometimes
has the impression that the entire Irish nation was
involved in the literary revival, its achievements, its
controversies and its arguments. The success of a play
was a victory for the whole country. When a play was
booed or disrupted, it seems as though the entire country
was in uproar. Dublin's literary life was, however, utterly
foreign to the peasants of Peter O'Leary's *My Story* and
Brinsley MacNamara's *The Valley of the Squinting
Windows*, just as it was to the inhabitants of Belfast's
industrial ghettos.

But the influence of writers is not simply a direct one
on their immediate audiences and readers: they also
affect influential people and contribute to the formation
of the sensitivity of a people through a series of relays
and transmissions. In Ireland, these intermediaries were
particularly numerous and active. Societies and organisations spreading ideas were many, and they used both
oral and written forms, the press, leaflets, pamphlets,
speeches, lectures and classes. So, though the wax of
Ireland which they wanted to mould had already
hardened, writers occupy an inordinately large space in
the memory of those years. The 1916 Rebellion is often
called the 'Poets' Revolution'; MacDonagh, Pearse and
Plunkett, three of the seven signatories of the
proclamation of the Republic, were poets. With the
passing of the years, Patrick Pearse has become an
almost mythological figure.[19]

The generally accepted idea is that the failure of the
political movement was compensated for by 'cultural
nationalism' – that is to say that the writers of the Irish
renaissance filled the political vacuum. It would be more
accurate to say, as Robert Kee does, that the cultural
revival coincided with the first waves of enthusiasm for
Home Rule and continued its development when the

political movement lost its attraction and subsided.[20] Many important manifestations of the literary and cultural revival occurred before the fall of Parnell and the ensuing political crisis. Numerous literary clubs and societies for research into the history of the country and into Gaelic literature and society were founded. These activities were still scattered and would take time to crystallise into a coherent whole but, from this time onwards, cultural organisations played an important part in attracting Irish people, including exiles, to the nationalist cause. Exiles, of course, had long been separated from Irish reality – though one sometimes wonders if those who had stayed behind were more familiar with 'reality'. The exiles remembered a mythical country and were delighted to encounter people and organisations who told them that their recollections could come true.

When Maud Gonne arrived in Dublin from France, eager to work for national liberation, she wanted to become a member of the Celtic Literary Society, but women were not eligible so she helped to found a society for women, the Daughters of Erin, whose aims were to

> re-establish the complete independence of Ireland; to encourage the study of Gaelic, of Irish literature, history, music and art ... to support and publicise Irish manufacture; to discourage the circulation of low English literature, the singing of English songs, the attending of vulgar English entertainments ... and to combat in every way any English influence.[21]

The cultural struggle dimension was not primarily intended to make Irish-Americans happy however. It provided a confidence and a sense of dignity for the Irish people. The following dialogue, taken from Brinsley MacNamara's *The Valley of the Squinting Windows*, will perhaps make this idea more comprehensible.

> He was fond of telling her about the younger Irish poets and of quoting passages from their poems. Now it would be a line or so from Colum or Stephens, again a verse from

Seamus O'Sullivan or Joseph Campbell. Continually he spoke with enthusiasm of the man they called AE ... She found it difficult to believe that such men could be living in Ireland at the present time.

'And would you see them about Dublin?'

'Yes, you'd see them often.'

'*Real* poets?'

'Real poets surely. But of course they have earthly interests as well. One is a farmer.'

'A farmer!!!'

This she found it hardest of all to believe, for the word 'farmer' made her see so clearly the sullen men with the dirty beards who came in the white roads every evening to drink in Garradrimna. There was no poetry in them.[22]

The characters having this conversation are Rebecca Kerr, a country schoolmistress, and Ulick Shannon, a medical student in Dublin, the son of a prosperous local farmer. It is impossible to credit the depths of despair and discouragement which people must have reached if a schoolmistress could no longer believe that men of letters existed in her own country. So, a farmer could be a poet and a poet could write about the peasantry. For the peasant masses, cut off as they were from schooling and education, the printed word was the symbol of social success: schoolmasters, the rich, civil servants and priests were all people who read.

The fall of Parnell, felt as a deep humiliation, had made this need for dignity all the more important. Charles Stewart Parnell had attained the status of 'Uncrowned King' of Ireland and enjoyed immense popularity. He was beyond dispute the prophet come to give Ireland back her past, her glory and her greatness; he made up for the Flight of the Earls, the defeat of James II by William of Orange and the Famine. Together with Daniel O'Connell, he picked up the threads of past greatness. To this day, arguments continue as to the historical and political importance of Daniel O'Connell, but on one point, at least, there is unanimity: he gave the Irish masses a new dignity, restored to them the feeling of their own strength. The Famine had been felt as divine curse, a punishment for too much pride, as the beginning of a long dark period. Then came Parnell, the Redeemer.

Parnell's fall was, therefore, the fall of the prophet, but at the same time a fall that had been brought about by the faithful themselves and owed nothing, it seemed, to the enemy without. He had been struck down by the Irish themselves; it was now up to the Irish to redeem themselves, to expunge their crime, to purge their shame by sacrificing themselves on the altar of Parnell. Young militants, in their search for their own Way of the Cross, quite naturally turned to the heirs of the Fenians and the tradition of physical force. Whilst waiting to take their place in the pantheon of martyrs, they kept their ardour alive by familiarising themselves with literary works which glorified the figure of Parnell and of his predecessors. Writers, for their part, were ready to play the role expected of them. They felt themselves borne aloft by Ireland's history. They believed in the purity and innocence of a peasant nation which they would fashion in their own way. They had before them the example of Thomas Davis and consciously set themselves the task of continuing his work and struggle, but not in exactly the same way, as they sensed its limitations and imperfections. The poetry of the Young Irelanders, grouped around the newspaper the *Nation* reflected the political movement too superficially. Their ambition was a higher one. Their poetry 'should create subtler values and humanise the political movement'.[23] Yeats dissociated himself endlessly from the Young Irelanders' literature. What they rejected was perfectly expressed by J. P. Dalton in a preface to *The Spirit of the Nation*:

> Any discussion of the poetic quality of the songs, either singly or in the gross, would here be out of place. The poets of the *Nation* ... had not as a body developed the apprentice stage of training in their command of the resources and the techniques that are essential to the attainment of mastery in feats of poetic effort. But we should bear in mind that these remarkable men cultivated poetry chiefly as an auxiliary in the cause and

service of patriotism, and that they never paid court to
the art as the prime object of their affections.

For this reason, *The Spirit of the Nation* is more than a
selection of poetry published in Thomas Davis's paper the
Nation, it is a 'national memorial'.[24] The use of the word
'remarkable' is itself remarkable. This phrase shows
clearly that these poets were extraordinary because they
refused to consider poetry as anything but an instrument
in the service of a patriotic cause. Members of the new
generation had other ambitions and did not simply want
to add more stones to the national memorial.

Apart from this more critical outlook, much more
important for the moment was the enduring cultural
importance of Thomas Davis. It actually seemed that the
state of Ireland at the end of the century had much in
common with Thomas Davis's Ireland of the 1840s. The
fall of Parnell was like an echo of the fall of Daniel
O'Connell. As in the period after the fall of 'The
Liberator', the Irish masses found themselves leaderless
and disorientated. The position was vacant and every
male poet, journalist or lawyer member of a nationalist
or cultural club saw himself as predestined to occupy his
place. The trumpets had to be sounded. A word was
needed to give the signal. That would be no problem –
was it not the job of a poet to transform the word into a
signal?

It was a two-way traffic. The poets wanted the status of
prophets, the Irish were waiting for a Messiah, and,
curiously enough, they were waiting for him to come from
outside. They were crushed by defeat and oppression to
such an extent that salvation could not come from among
their own numbers. Return from exile, far from being an
obstacle, was another point in favour of would-be
saviours. In Dublin the welcome given to poets living on
the Continent and returning to take part in the cultural
renaissance was enthusiastic. The return of the
intellectual aristocracy became part of the Return of the
Earls, the return of the 'Wild Geese', driven out by the

English, whom ballads and prayers had at last managed to bring back to their native land.

This waiting for the Messiah is to be found in the names popularly given to political leaders. Daniel O'Connell was 'The Counsellor', 'The Agitator', 'The Liberator'; Parnell was 'The Uncrowned King'. The death of Parnell fitted perfectly into popular mythology: like Christ he died to save Irish people and like Christ he would rise again.

One of the major dilemmas for the 'poets' was how to reconcile the role of prophet – of which they dreamed – and their literary desire to overturn a certain number of prejudices. How were they going to change the outlook of the mass of the population and also become their leaders? How could they be both popular and avant-garde?

They reconciled their contradictions rather unsatisfactorily. Their models for influencing the masses were indeed those of O'Connell and Parnell, but O'Connell's and Parnell's power was due to their development and exploitation of themes inspired by dominant and generally accepted ideas, whilst the intellectuals advocated notions of 'quality' and of critical thought, that is the constant re-examination of dominant ideas. They dreamed of an audience which would be both popular and discriminating. This was a profound misunderstanding, because they were being asked to formulate popular aspirations, in their existing state, and above all, to refrain from attacking them head-on. All the requirements for stormy relationship were here present.

Notes

1 R.F. Foster, *Modern Ireland, 1600–1972*, London 1988, p. 431.
2 John Hutchinson, *The Gaelic Revival and the Creation of the Irish Nation State*, London 1987.
3 Eamon de Valera, 'The Values of the Spirit', 6 February 1933, in Maurice Moynihan (ed.), *Speeches and Statements by de Valera, 1917–1973*, Dublin 1980.
4 Lennox Robinson, *Ireland's Abbey Theatre*, London 1951, pp. 32–3.
5 Sean O'Faolain, 'The Stuffed Shirts', *Bell*, June 1943.

6 C. Desmond Greaves, *Liam Mellows and the Irish Revolution*, London 1971, p. 167.

7 'Red Hand', *Through Corruption to Dismemberment, A Story of Apostasy and Betrayal*, Derry, n.d.

8 Malcolm Brown, *The Politics of Irish Literature, from Thomas Davis to W.B. Yeats*, London 1972, p. 27.

9 Ernie O'Malley, *On Another Man's Wound*, Tralee 1979, p. 6.

10 Ibid., p. 15.

11 Ibid., p. 40.

12 Ibid., p. 56.

13 De Valera speaking in the Dail, 29 April 1932, in Moynihan (ed.), op. cit.

14 De Valera speaking in the Dail, 12 July 1928, in ibid.

15 De Valera, radio broadcast, 17 March 1943, in ibid.

16 Franco Venturi, *Les Intellectuels, le Peuple et la Révolution, Histoire du Populisme Russe au 19ème Siècle*, Paris 1972. Vol. I, p. 166.

17 W.B. Yeats, *Autobiographies, Reveries Over Childhood and Youth*, London 1970, p. 101.

18 D.F. McCarthy in *The Spirit of the Nation*, Dublin 1934 (originally published 1845).

19 See, for example, Herbert Howarth, *Literature Under Parnell's Star*, London 1958, Richard Loftus, *Nationalism in Modern Anglo-Irish Poetry*, Wisconsin 1964, John Jordan, 'Pearse and Yeats', *Hibernia*, 27 April 1973, Tom Garvin, *Nationalist Revolutionaries in Ireland 1858–1928*, Oxford 1987.

20 Robert Kee, *The Green Flag, A History of Irish Nationalism*, London 1972, p. 427.

21 Anne Marecco, *The Rebel Countess, The Life and Times of Constance Markievicz*, London 1967, p. 106.

22 Brinsley MacNamara, *The Valley of the Squinting Windows*, Tralee 1968, p. 100 (first published 1918).

23 Howarth, op. cit.

24 J.P. Dalton, preface to 1927 edition of *The Spirit of the Nation*, Dublin 1927, pp. 5–6.

1 Cultural Models

George Russell, an Ulster-born intellectual, was one of the key figures in the literary revival who wrote under the *nom de plume* 'AE'. His essay 'Nationality and Cosmopolitanism in Art' is fundamental for an understanding of the movement.

> Nationality was never so strong in Ireland as at the present time. It is beginning to be felt, less as a political movement than as a spiritual force. It seems to be gathering itself together, joining men who were hostile before, in a new intellectual fellowship: and if all these could unite on fundamentals it would be possible in a generation to create a national ideal in Ireland ... the spirit ... which ... whispered through the lips of the bards and peasant story-tellers.
>
> Every Irishman forms some vague ideal of his country born from his reading of history, or from contemporary politics, or from an imaginative intuition; and this Ireland in the mind is not the actual Ireland which kindles his enthusiasm. For this he works and makes sacrifices; but ... the ideal remains vague ... To reveal Ireland in clear and beautiful light, to create the Ireland in the heart, is the province of national literature.[1]

This passage summarises exactly what Ernie O'Malley meant by the 'lyrical stage' of national consciousness:

> Without guidance or direction, moving as if to clarify itself, nebulous, forming, reforming, the strange rebirth took shape. It was manifest in flags, badges, songs, speech, all seemingly superficial signs. It was as if the inarticulate attempted to express themselves ... later would come organisation and cool-headed reason. Now

was the lyrical stage, blood sang and pulsed, a strange
love was born that for some was never to die till they lay
stiff on the hillside or in quicklime near a barrack wall.[2]

No single text can be taken as the manifesto of the
Irish cultural renaissance for the simple reason that too
many writers tried to write their own manifesto, but AE's
'Nationality and Cosmopolitanism in Art' is nevertheless
one of the most revealing and lucid of such declarations.

The Irish all have their own opinion about their
country and it is this ideal which upholds their
nationalist enthusiasm – the ideal, not Irish reality.
Unlike many other authors, George Russell did not
confuse illusion and reality, did not reduce his country to
the mythological idealisation made of it by others. He
was, indeed, quite clear that this idealisation was more
important than reality. It is not history which makes
people act, but legends. 'They have now the character of
symbols and, as symbols, are more potent than history.'[3]

The object of the literary revival was therefore to gather
together all the bits and pieces of this mythology into a
coherent whole and to make Ireland the Mecca for all
nations with aspirations to national independence. These
conclusions deserve to be studied more closely as they did
not emanate from a prisoner in the realm of ideas. AE
played an active and practical role in organisations such
as the Irish Agricultural Organisation Society, the object
of which was to increase the number of agricultural co-
operatives in the country. But the 'rural society' which he
wanted to build was based on a cultural conception of his
country. For George Russell, the task of organising peasant communities and the activity of literary societies were
all part of the same whole, the former, indeed, being a
guarantee of the latter's success.[4]

The terms of reference are based on the Gaelic legend
of the Ireland of scholars and poets, and it is striking to
note the degree to which the description of that idyllic
period in the history of the country was written to serve
as an example to the contemporary intelligentsia.

Gaelic Ireland

The picture of the ancient bards which emerged in Ireland at the end of the nineteenth century was not new. It was based on a good deal of research and translation from Gaelic, the results of which were amplified by European Romanticism.[5] The best known exposition of this ideal past is Daniel Corkery's book *The Hidden Ireland* in which the dominant sentiment is the compulsion to reveal that which had been unknown, scorned and belittled, but which was nevertheless the soul of the nation. The poets of Gaelic society and the language in which they expressed themselves were both considered as unimportant and unworthy of attention. None the less, they embodied the continuity of a national identity:

> a country where for some 1,500 years, as far back as historic knowledge can reach, one national force has overshadowed and dominated all others. It has been the power of a great literary tradition.[6]

De Valera was to stress the idea that, 'The Irish genius has always stressed spiritual and intellectual rather than material values.' Historians, Daniel Corkery claimed, have ignored that unique tradition which guaranteed national continuity. They have become attached to the city, to Dublin and the Ascendancy, and turned their backs on the greater part of Ireland – the Gaelic-speaking peasantry – those who the foreigners called 'domestic enemies' or 'the savage old Irish'. They have reduced Ireland's history to its parliamentary, constitutional and aristocratic elements.

The ancient Ireland which inspired the poets of the literary revival was presented as a close-knit, harmonious world in which different social groups were united by the same culture in which all foreign influences were hostile and destructive. Nobles spoke Irish to their servants. The children of the aristocracy were brought up by peasants who passed on to them the Irish language, legends and culture. 'Those big houses, when Gaelic, shared a common culture with the lowly peasant's hut.'[7]

The nobles were the protectors and patrons of the poets. The bards therefore sang about their virtues and their feats of arms, and composed poems celebrating the achievements of the nobility from the cradle to the grave. This way of life was destroyed by an invasion which brought with it poverty, famine and an end to this idyllic relationship. The nobles, fallen on hard times, found themselves on the same level as their peasants. The poets, in the midst of their poverty, could still claim noble descent. The industrial revolution accentuated still further the destruction of a communal way of life. Many poems in the eighteenth century lament the destruction of the old forests – the wood had gone to be burned in England or to be used as pit-props. The destruction of the forests and the destruction of Gaelic society went hand in hand in these laments.

In spite of the destruction of the peasant way of life and the protective 'Big House', the soul of Ireland survived thanks to the poet who was the central character of this society. He was a privileged person. Trained in the bardic schools, which were really the nation's universities, he occupied a hereditary official position which was reached at the end of a lengthy apprenticeship based on the history of the country and that of the clan to which he belonged. His social status was due to his knowledge of the language and history. As we shall see, this training programme described by Daniel Corkery resembles the requirements laid down by Arthur Griffith and Sinn Fein for future civil servants.

Only the descendants of poets could be admitted to the bardic schools grouped around the teacher, who alone was responsible for the school's renown. There were no fixed buildings – where the teacher found himself, there was the school.

One should be very careful of interpreting a text with the benefit of hindsight, but it does seem that Daniel Corkery's emphasis on the social status of the 'fili' expressed strongly the aspirations of the educated classes. This chimes perfectly with Arthur Griffith's *Sinn Fein Policy*, a complete cultural programme which was published in 1905. Access to culture allows one to avoid the hard facts of agricultural work and the dispossessed landowners refused to do servile work which they considered as an 'intolerable insult'.

> Pleasant the scholar's life
> When his books surround him ...
> Early rising, shepherding
> These he never yields,
> And just as little worries him
> Tillage or watching in the night.[8]

After the destruction of the Gaelic order of things, the social status of the poets declined rapidly. It is probably at this period that the fallen 'fili' place most emphasis on their past glories. Their 'pleasant life' had never seemed so agreeable to them as when it was vanishing. Impoverished and reduced to wandering through the countryside in semi-clandestine conditions, they sang nostalgically about their past glory. Their first vindication was to be through Thomas Davis's movement and the Young Irelanders gathered around the *Nation*.

The *Nation* or Poetry as a Weapon

> Nothing so surely tells us of the desperateness of their cause that the name of no political leader of their own is found in their songs from the fall of Limerick to the rise of O'Connell – a wilderness of more than a hundred years.[9]

For Daniel Corkery, Wolfe Tone was not to be considered as a 'political leader', no doubt because he could not forgive the rebellious Protestant his dislike of traditional singing and mores. Daniel O'Connell is a hero more to his heart, and with his arrival Ireland awoke, shook off a long period of passivity and showed her strength. The poets rediscovered both their country and the hero who personified it.

Daniel O'Connell, a Catholic lawyer from a prosperous County Kerry family, was a good representative of the group of Catholics for whom emancipation meant new possibilities for advancement. His relations with the peasantry, although they prefigured modern mass parties, were more of a religious than of a political nature. The framework he reconstituted was that of the peasant masses guided by the aristocrat, the 'natural' leader. Most important, of course, was that hundreds of thousands of Irish people had their experience of political activity as a result of O'Connell's campaigns. Though most of them were not to be included in the franchise following emancipation, they built up day-by-day a store of lessons which were to be invaluable in the future.

One aspect of such lessons that bears directly on this work was about the relationship between Daniel O'Connell, the politician, and Thomas Davis, the poet who co-founded the *Nation*. The image left by Daniel O'Connell is that of a man who personified all the virtues and all the faults of the Irish people. He was a Celt and a Catholic, he knew how to arouse the support of the masses with his speeches. His movement was sectarian, which is to say it had the support of the Catholic church. He had an abiding hatred of revolution and took great care to isolate the Irish from foreign radical movements, whether the French Revolution or English Chartism. He laid great emphasis on the non-violent aspect of his methods. Daniel O'Connell was talking to Catholics, and his speeches were aimed at the peasant masses.

Thomas Davis, a Protestant lawyer and graduate of Trinity College, repeated Wolfe Tone's appeals to all the religions in Ireland, but primarily to the Protestant aristocracy and, in a more general way, to the cultured elite of the nation.[11] Daniel O'Connell stood for material things, the soil, the masses; Thomas Davis stood for the spirit, culture, the elite. Daniel O'Connell wanted to give a share of political power to well-to-do Catholics. Thomas

Davis wanted to give a soul to his country. Daniel O'Connell made his compatriots act; Thomas Davis asked them to educate themselves, to learn the history of their country, to sing and paint the heroes of the past.

Thomas Davis's tradition, as it was passed down to the generation of 1916, was always seen in the light of a confrontation between the two men. Davis acted as a goad. He represented the national mystique against Daniel O'Connell who had soiled the national cause with his attention to material and political concerns. Through his poetry, Davis appeared as the enemy of compromise. Daniel O'Connell turned away from shedding blood, while it flowed freely in Davis's poetic imagery. Words were useless without the flashing swords of the Irish Volunteers.[11] Davis was thus isolated from the popular movement which had inspired him. One only remembered the impassioned songs and the magical words which Daniel O'Connell was reproached for not having used to the full:

> Davis' songs came to be regarded as pure wizardry. Irishmen in later times, especially when hard-pressed in retreat, listened for the magician who, with only a verse or two and a couple of old airs, could turn the tide of their disasters. In storm and doldrums alike, the air was to be filled with warlike incantations in the hope of once again raising up the hordes of ready men who had gathered at Tara.[12]

As if Davis's cultural nationalism could be separated from the political movement which inspired it. The *Nation* had a circulation of 25,000, and it was estimated that each copy of the paper was read – or heard in public readings – by ten people. This success can only be explained by Daniel O'Connell's support, and the paper faithfully reported all the Chief's speeches.

Daniel O'Connell knew how to use the strength and the threat of mass pressure. He knew how to lead people on and how to hold them back. He knew how to use the threat of armed revolt whilst at the same time declaring that he detested violence. Nothing was more distasteful to him than social revolution, and he advocated the union of all classes of society to achieve aims which would eventually exclude the lower orders. Such contradictions cannot be resolved harmoniously when political power is at stake. How was he to rally both landowners and tenants with whom they were at daggers drawn? Thomas Davis's poetry was able to supply an imagery common to all these groups, to fuse the diverse aims into a broad nationalist sentiment. Landlords who were demanding new laws against agrarian terrorism and the peasants who were terrorising the landowners could be 'be brothers in a common patriotism'. In these circumstances, vagueness was the most important virtue in the arsenal of symbolism.[13]

The contradiction in the methods used could itself also be resolved in poetry. To use the threat of armed violence to the full, while at the same time fearing it like the plague, the best solution is to give it an entirely literary expression, in which drum-rolls, flashing swords and gunfire do not cause a single drop of blood to flow.

O'Connell's order to back down from the threatened 'monster meeting' at Clontarf in 1843 could only have been given in prose, so when the eternal rebels condemned the 'cowardice' of 'The Liberator' they naturally turned to the call to arms expressed in the poetry of Thomas Davis.

The Fenians or Poetry under Arms

The crisis which followed the fall of Daniel O'Connell and the death of Thomas Davis was a profound one. The Young Irelanders were open to attack, at the same moment deprived of their spiritual leader and the invaluable contact with the common people which O'Connell had given them. Those who were left, Gavan Duffy, John Mitchel and M.J. Barry, were joined by new recruits, mainly young Catholics from the middle classes. They emphasised still further the tendency for the movement to become inward-looking, prey to internal dissension and wedded to a language that was divorced from reality. The more the Young Irelanders were separated from the ordinary people of Ireland, their day-to-day struggles and their social and cultural reality, the more they tried to compensate for this by the vehement affirmation of that patriotism of which they considered themselves to be the exclusive guardians.

The Great Famine found the Young Irelanders completely disarmed and powerless – and infuriated by their powerlessness. The most ecstatic dreams of emancipation crumbled in the face of agricultural cataclysm. The Young Irelanders continued their 'attack' either in speeches or in pathetic revolts. According to the lessons they had learned, or rather, that they had taught, the Irish people could not allow itself to die of hunger. The people *had* to revolt. It only needed one spark to bring the guns and pikes out of the barns. The French revolution of 1848 inflamed the Young Irelanders' minds. At a time when hundreds of thousands of people were dying or being weakened by famine, John Mitchel was giving instructions for street combat:

Windows, brickbats, heavy furniture, logs of wood and pokers were to be cast down on the heads of the troops; cavalry, the inhabitants of Dublin were told, cannot charge over broken bottles, and vitriol, boiling water and boiling grease were also to be poured from above on the troops' heads. Soldiers were to be tempted into narrow streets where such methods would have their maximum effect.[14]

The split came about with the bungled rebellion. William Smith O'Brien gathered together 6,000 men at Mullinahone. The next morning, the crowd of combatants had considerably diminished. They had come in the hope of getting food, and went away again when they discovered that they were expected to fend for themselves. Smith O'Brien's declarations after the defeat savagely reveal the blindness of the Young Irelanders:

It matters little whether the blame of failure lies on me or
upon others; but the fact is recorded in our annals – that
the people preferred to die of starvation at home, or flee as
voluntary exiles to other lands, rather than to fight for
their lives and liberties.[15]

These well-fed men, who were used to spending the
winter months in less harsh climates, could not imagine
that the future and ambition of an entire people could be
reduced to a pound of flour. They felt personally betrayed
and could only conceive of the passive wanderings of the
Irish peasantry in terms of choice, that is to say of guilt.

These traits would manifest themselves on a larger
scale in the Fenian movement. Successive failures,
isolation from the conflicts of the masses and from their
everyday reality, the romanticism to which secret
societies gave rise – all these contributed to a
dramatisation of political struggle. The form of combat
and the beauty of the gesture took over from the search
for precise objectives. The struggles and discussions took
place in an apparently closed world, one into which the
kind of history which changes people and the
relationships between them did not penetrate. Reading
the jail journals of the great Fenian leaders, one
wonders, as many of their contemporaries did, whether,
after all, the history of Ireland was not made without
them – perhaps even in spite of them. Beaten men,
outlaws, prisoners and exiles, their history is a series of
bungled insurrections and flamboyant speeches, but all
the while, and unnoticed by them, Ireland was changing.
Those changes, moreover, were in total contradiction to
the Fenians' own predictions.

Contact with insurrection was harsh and disappoint-
ing. The Fenian leaders theorised about their successive
defeats and transformed them into victories. The Fenian
movement did not succeed in knitting together the
threads of great popular objectives. Isolation was to be
glorified and transformed into a virtue. These difficulties
were not resolved but sanctified. Isolation and defeat
became the supreme guarantee of good faith in the

national struggle. The latter had been emptied of all content. It had to be 'pure' of all outside demands. The liberation of Ireland was like the search for the Holy Grail – it was the only objective which nothing could soil: 'No amount of good government could be a substitute for self-government, and the pursuit of particular reforms, even reform of the land-system, was a dangerous heresy.'[16]

This distinction was well expressed by John O'Leary, one of the Fenian leaders, when he protested against confusing Fenians and Ribbonmen. The Ribbonmen were members of an agrarian secret society whose terrorist activities were directed against landlords and Protestants, while the Fenians constituted a nationalist movement which was exclusively anti-English.[17]

The search for purity was also to be found in the methods used. The Fenian movement had an organisation, a strategy and tactics which were essentially military. Just as the demands of the peasantry and of the working class, whether economic or political, risked soiling the purity of the national struggles, any military method which did not involve the supreme sacrifice was unworthy of the ideal to be attained. The right way of saying things was of no value compared with the art of fighting. John Devoy tells how he was recruited into the secret society. Not unnaturally, another member wanted to test Devoy's patriotism before having him sworn in – 'a wholly unnecessary proceeding, for I already belonged to a gun club'.[18] All Patrick Pearse's writings and speeches on the necessity for sacrifice and bloodshed had been foreshadowed in Fenian tracts. Pearse had learnt his Mitchel well:

> Before there can be any general arming or aptitude to insurrection there must first be sound manly doctrine preached and embraced. And next, there must be many desultory collisions with British troops, both in town and country and the sight of clear steel and of blood smoking hot must become familiar to the eyes of men, of boys and women.[19]

For the Fenians, defeat never had political causes, but
was always a purely military defeat. For Devoy, past
insurrections had failed 'because of lack of the essentials
of military success: trained men, educated officers, arms
and ammunition'.[20] Writing about James Stephens's
refusal to give the order for an insurrection, John Devoy
threw aside the political reasons for this refusal: 'The
chief question was most certainly a military one, and it
was decided by a civilian, against the judgement and
advice of his military advisers.'[21]

This affirmation was strengthened by the fact that the
military advisers in question were American officers who
had distinguished themselves in the American Civil War.
It was sufficient to have had military experience to be
able to lead; the specific nature of that experience did not
seem to count for much. John Devoy joined the French
Foreign Legion and Thomas Clarke Luby also wanted to
join the French army in order to learn infantry tactics. It
would hard to make a greater separation between the
means used and the nature of the struggle.

Given the circumstances, a military victory was
inevitably confined to the imagination. Defeats were
therefore transformed into heroic exploits and exemplary
sacrifices. With only a few notable exceptions, such as
James Stephens's *The Insurrection of Dublin*, the
declarations and books which came out of the Easter
Rising were a celebration of a great feat of arms, of the
courage of the combatants and the heroism of the
martyrs. The reader of these accounts could be forgiven
for failing to realise that this rebellion was actually
defeated on the Republicans' home ground – the
battlefield. The political consequences were different, but
military defeat was military defeat. A comparison with
another major uprising may help to clarify this point.
The Paris Commune is remembered and commemorated
by revolutionaries in France and all over the world. But
in the years which followed 1870, socialists did not hide
the fact that the Parisian uprising ended in serious
defeat, that many of the city's most promising

working-class leaders had been massacred. On the contrary, it was in trying to explain this defeat, so as to avoid a similar one in the future, that French socialist leaders were able to rebuild their organisations.

In the case of the Fenian writers, the mere fact of having fought, or having taken up their arms, was already a victory. There was no need to look for reasons for the defeat since defeat did not exist. In John Devoy's memoirs, this idea is repeated in every chapter. He explains the failure of the 1798 insurrection by the over-large part played by civilians in a purely military affair.[22] He compares that failure with other battles. Hugh O'Neill in his campaign against Elizabeth had a well-trained army, but Devoy does not say that it was defeated. Owen Roe O'Neill fought magnificently against Cromwell because he had the help of 200 experienced officers who had come from Spain, but the final rout is not mentioned. The peak is reached in his comments on the war against William of Orange:

> [The Irish] had a small but well-trained force ... And they might, by enlisting a larger force, have won in the end but for the cowardice, avarice and treachery of the English King in whose cause they wasted their valor.[23]

Which amounts to saying that they would have won had they been fighting on the other side. Armed combat was not only the supreme form of fighting for independence – it was the *only* form of combat: 'We were confronted with the alternative of doing something desperate or giving up the hope of a fight for some time.'[24]

Military art was the apogee of political commitment, thus sanctifying failure, and the natural outcome was the eternal praising of heroes fallen on the field. Death is the supreme military victory, funeral ceremonies their finest celebration. The burial of Terence Bellew MacManus played a decisive role in the launching of the Fenian movement; later, that of O'Donovan Rossa, at which Patrick Pearse delivered his famous oration, did the same for the Easter Rising. The obsequies of a hero are as good a training as any for learning to march in step:

> The men in line were of fine physique and their splendid bearing greatly impressed the English newspapermen. The latter thought they had all been drilled but Irishmen are born soldiers and fall into military step naturally.[25]

But how could a purely military movement give a privileged place to writers and intellectuals? The majority of Fenian militants were from humble backgrounds – small farmers, labourers, artisans, primary-school teachers and shop-assistants. A young rebel in the 1850s was naturally attracted by the Fenians.[26] Nevertheless, the leaders and officers belonged to the middle and upper classes. A poet was not necessarily a good commander, but a good commander had to have a certain level of education and culture. 'O'Reilly became a poet of considerable worth in America. Nevertheless he had the spirit of a good military leader.'[27] We should bear in mind how Devoy described the model army which Ireland needed: 'trained men, educated officers'. The reasons for this are an integral part of the Fenian movement. When there are no real battles going on, only sham ones, when long and monotonous war is replaced by a series of warlike declarations and desperate deeds, then the poet has every chance of succeeding.

The whole ideology of the Fenian movement demanded that the leaders should be the very cream, the chosen few, of the fight for liberty. Every member of the Fenian leadership considered himself to be just that: an irreplaceable charismatic, the brain and inspiration of his troops. They were the chosen few because of the way in which they had joined the struggle. At a given moment in their lives, they had received the grace, had been converted in the religious sense of the term. John O'Leary, while he was convalescing from an illness, started to read Thomas Davis's essays and poems. He describes the transformation he underwent as a process analogous with that which many Christians call 'conversion'.[28] However, it would seem that this type of conversion was only possible for men of a certain culture and social standing. O'Leary praised the artisan class: 'It is in this class that I have always found the best Irishmen. [They] are ... more intelligent ... more cultured than any,' but, he immediately added, 'save the professional and professedly cultured class'.[29]

Culture and education are constant reference-points. Stephens was an engineer. John O'Mahoney is described as 'an Irishman of the old school, with a superb physique, well-educated and perfectly literate in Irish'[30] and Devoy adds, almost as an extra title of nobility, that O'Mahoney had translated Keating's *History of Ireland* into English. John O'Leary thought that no one deserved to be a leader unless he had received a higher education. Thomas Clarke Luby was a man of enormous literary talent and highly cultured. Charles Kickham was a writer, novelist and poet. Thomas J. Clarke explains that an educated man, whose head is full of ideas, runs less risk of breaking down in prison than an uneducated man.[31] All these men were, to use John Devoy's expression, 'armed poets'.[32] Doubtless one could study the Fenian movement as a work of art, as a collective creation constantly retouched and modified by artists searching for the most perfect form of expression. The quest for purity in the national struggle became a kind of aestheticism; pushed to its extreme, the struggle was never so 'pure' as when it was not actually taking place:

> The Fenians were self-sacrificing men ... That is why the movement which missed the chance to show heroism on the battlefield and had no military victories to its account has exercised such a profound influence on the Irish people.[33]

The Fenian leaders certainly experienced hardship, prison and exile. When they spoke and wrote of the supreme sacrifice, this was not just an idle boast. In spite of everything, today their memoirs read like the diaries of veteran fighters in an ideal war which did not take place.

It is none the less true that they created a world in which poetry had a distinct smell of gunpowder. The myth will survive. In Sean O'Casey's *Shadow of a Gunman*, the poet is of necessity a freedom fighter. But being the shadow of a gunman, he is also the shadow of a poet.

Notes

1   AE (G.W. Russell), 'Nationality and Cosmopolitanism in Art' in *Some Irish Essays*, Dublin 1906, pp. 12–13.
2   Ernie O'Malley, *On Another Man's Wound*, Tralee 1979, pp. 41–2.
3   AE, op. cit., p. 18.
4   AE, *The Building up of a Rural Civilisation*, Dublin 1910.
5   Patrick Rafroidi, *L'Irlande et le Romantisme*, Paris 1972, Part 2 Ch.5.
6   Stopford Green in Daniel Corkery, *The Hidden Ireland*, Dublin 1970, p. 69.
7   Corkery, op. cit., p. 61.
8   Ibid., p. 85.
9   Ibid.
10   Robert Kee, *The Green Flag, A History of Irish Nationalism*, London 1972, pp. 193–202, Malcolm Brown, *The Politics of Irish Literature, From Thomas Davis to W.B. Yeats*, London 1972, p. 41.
11   *The Spirit of the Nation*, Dublin 1934, p. 38.
12   Brown, op. cit., p. 72.
13   Ibid., p. 55.
14   Cecil Woodham-Smith, *The Great Hunger*, London 1963.
15   Ibid., pp. 356–7.
16   T.W. Moody, 'The Fenian Movement in Irish History' in T.W. Moody (ed.), *The Fenian Movement*, Cork 1968, p. 104.
17   John O'Leary, *Recollections of Fenians and Fenianism*, London 1896.
18   John Devoy, *Recollections of an Irish Rebel*, New York 1929, p. 26.
19   John Mitchel, *Jail Journal*, Dublin 1918, p. 128.
20   Devoy, op. cit., p. 128.
21   Ibid., p. 96.
22   Ibid., Ch. XIX.
23   Ibid., p. 130.
24   Ibid., p. 108.
25   Ibid., p. 24.
26   Moody, op. cit.
27   O'Leary, op. cit.
28   O'Leary, op. cit., p. 30.
29   Ibid.
30   Devoy, op. cit., p. 266.
31   Thomas J. Clarke, *Glimpses of an Irish Felon's Prison Life*, Dublin and London 1922.
32   Devoy, op. cit., p. 289.
33   Ibid., pp. 319–20.

2 Eloquent and Wealthy

What Sean O'Faolain called the putsch of the middle classes was not, in fact so much a putsch as a well organised, gradual and generally accepted rise and coming-to-power of people who had, because of a colonial situation, previously been excluded from political power.[1] It was, in fact, the reverse of a putsch: putsches or coups are the action of a minority of people, and tend to come as a surprise. The transfer of power in Ireland was slow and endorsed by successive elections and mass demonstrations. The books, plays and pamphlets that announced it were maybe not taken very seriously at the time, but, with the benefit of hindsight, it is clear that they outlined a political programme that was faithfully carried out.

The Ethics of Sinn Fein, published as a pamphlet by the National Council of Sinn Fein in Dublin in September 1917, is dominated by the emphasis placed on the individual rather than on adhesion to a social group or class. Independence is first and foremost a personal matter. The Sinn Feiner's moral obligations are many and restrictive. The pamphlet is addressed to an exclusively male readership as the Sinn Feiner was, by definition, a man. His conduct must be above reproach, his personality stainless. He must learn the Irish language, write on Irish paper, abstain from alcohol and tobacco.[2] This alone, however, was not enough. He must integrate all these moral decisions into the *personal* decision to break with England. Sinn Fein (Ourselves Alone) became Me Fein (Myself Alone). Do not depend on

others. The great army of the undependable included not
only the entire English race and the Irish deputies in
Westminster but also those involved in mass political
activities to which the Irish might be tempted to delegate
their will for independence – what the pamphlet called
'the old superstition according to which Ireland will be
saved by committees, by monster meetings, by exciting
elections'.[3]

The first duty of a patriot was to make Ireland a
nation. However, the only part of Ireland which a patriot
was able to liberate immediately was himself. A bad
patriot is he who waits until an independent state
organises Irish classes and Irish schools, who waits for
Ireland to be saved by a minister for education, by
elections, by people other than himself. To free Ireland,
one individual who actually learns the national language
was worth more than ninety-nine who wrote and made
speeches in English on the necessity for learning it.

In effect, each individual represented the Irish nation
in miniature. The distancing of each individual from
English influence in his conscience and being was a
distancing which benefited the whole nation.

> If you wish to see Ireland become a perfect country, a
> kingdom of God, do you yourself become a perfect
> individual, a kingdom of God. The perfect country can
> only be established by individual men and women, who
> are striving after perfection – perfection not only in an
> imaginary Irish nation which is within themselves, in
> their own brains and hearts and sinews, to mar or to
> make beautiful as they will.[4]

Set a good example: your virtue, your courage, your
temperance and your manliness will attract your fellow
countrymen to the national cause, including those who
are still hostile to it, such as Northern Unionists. These
are the people who must be convinced by example and
not the English, who are simply to be ignored – they have
nothing to do with Ireland's internal affairs.

> We must show that patriotism is a beautiful and noble thing and the surest way in which we can do this is to let it be seen that it has beautiful effects in our lives.[5]

The heroes of the past must not only be the object of respect and veneration, they must inspire every moment of our lives. We must all be Robert Emmetts and Thomas Davises. The ending perfectly sums up the pamphlet's spirit: 'The only way to be a patriotic Irishman is to do your best to become a perfect man.'[6]

Ironically, this idea of dividing the nation into male individuals, of making the individual a microcosm of society as a whole, comes directly from English political thinking of the seventeenth and eighteenth centuries. Developing considerably later in Ireland, its conservative traits are all the more clearly revealed. It favours the individual above the social. It hides privileges behind moral recommendations. Personal choice is revealed in the end as a luxury accessible only to a fraction of society. Individual morality betrays itself at times:

> It is your right to compel your tailor, if he is unwilling, to make your coat of Irish cloth, to compel your grocer to sell you Irish eggs, to compel your public servants to acquire some knowledge of the Irish language and help Irish industries.[7]

This is hardly the kind of advice one could give to an audience of small farmers or Dublin tenement dwellers – in other words the majority of the Irish people. How on earth could they 'oblige' their tailors to make their suits out of Irish cloth? They might just as well be asked to travel in a carriage 'made in Ireland'. Contrary to the assertion repeated throughout the pamphlet, it is not up to every Irishman to give his loyalty to the national cause. This advice is directed at middle-class, educated Irishmen, who as a result of knowledge, education or training, through their possession of economic resources or their place in the administrative hierarchy, have the means to pay, to educate and to lead the population. They are being asked to play the role of guides. In return, they are promised a fine future and possibilities for promotion which at the time were denied them by the English presence. 'The destinies of Ireland are in the hands of the free and noblemen and women of Ireland whom you can persuade, but could never compel to join you.'[8] Could it be clearer that an elite was being addressed?

This profoundly middle-class nature of the nationalist movements, which has left such a deep impression on the country, is shown even more clearly in cultural movements such as the Gaelic League, founded to revive the national language. *Facts About the Irish Language and the Irish Language Movements* purports to demonstrate to the Irish overseas and visitors to the country the effect of the Gaelic revival.[9] These effects are firstly the 'moral improvement of the lower classes'. The general tone of the pamphlet is that of a 'Lady Bountiful' and could well be the report of a temperance society or a group dedicated to the encouragement of thrift and virtue in working-class areas. The Gaelic League is cheering on the workers:

> In districts where the Gaelic League flourishes and its classes are well attended, the Technical Construction Lectures ... are well attended too. On the other hand, in localities where the people are so 'practical' that they 'will not waste time learning Irish' it is generally found that they have no inclination to learn better ways of butter-making or to adopt improvements in agricultural methods either.[10]

The Gaelic League encouraged temperance and enforced a strict ban on the sale of any kind of alcohol at its outdoor festivities, and no League meeting could 'take place in a house where liquor is sold'.[11] It tried to give the Irish more respectable tastes in their leisure activities and worked against vulgar entertainment and degrading shows.

> A few years ago Irishmen and Irishwomen were content to listen to with patience, and even to applaud plays and songs in which their country, their dress, their accent

were held up to ridicule; such things would not be tolerated in Ireland today.[12]

The domination of the Irish language movement by the urban intelligentsia who aimed to carry the good news into the countryside has been noted by a number of writers, but the implications of this middle-class character of the movement have not been taken up. When one thinks of the appalling state of poverty which reigned in Dublin tenements, and the state of material and cultural deprivation of the peasant masses, one is struck by the blindness of the Gaelic League militants when faced with social problems. 'Blindness' is perhaps the wrong word, as this state of affairs could not have escaped anyone's notice. It would be more accurate to say that they were incapable of dealing with this collective misery except in terms of morality and individual conduct. The industrial and cultural revival of the country was thought of in terms of personal redemption. The ideology of Victorian philanthropy was accepted in its entirety. The individual has to pay the price of tolerated oppression, passive slavery and the giving up of national traditions, by effort and self-sacrifice, by aiming at the highest moral virtues. The gap between these teachers of morality and the living conditions of the mass of the population was deep. Demanding personal reform was the exorbitant price set for their participation in the national struggle. It was as though the mass of the Irish were regarded as incapable of governing themselves as long as they had not demonstrated their spirit of self-sacrifice. The Gaelic League had not yet learned that one cannot teach a language to a child dying of starvation. First it has to be fed, even if it asks for food in English. As James Connolly observed:

> You cannot teach starving men Gaelic; and the treasury of our national literature will and must remain lost forever to the poor wage-slaves who are contented by our system to toil from early morning to late at night for a mere starvation wage.[13]

The idea of a mystical nation which would gather together all classes and all social groups is sometimes presented as an elaborate mask for a political plan first and foremost concerned with the interests of the Irish middle classes. Why on earth should it be called 'a mask'? True, cultural nationalism, by the vagueness and ambiguity of its expression, allowed for such distortion, but the political documents of the period did not conceal anything. The meaning of Sinn Fein doctrine, as expounded by Arthur Griffith, is perfectly clear. The pamphlet begins with another idea taken directly from eighteenth-century English philosophers: the Irish people are a free people and no one can alienate this freedom without a freely-taken decision. If the people decide otherwise, they have the sacred right to oppose any tyranny that a foreign power tries to impose. 'The first duty of the citizen is to oppose this tyranny and seek to put an end to it.'[14]

The first and most important means used by England to impose her tyranny on the Irish people is the educational system at all levels – primary, secondary and higher. Although Griffith accords some importance to the economic aspects of freedom, it is none the less 'cultural tyranny' that is given pride of place: 'Next in importance to the education question in this country is the question of our industries.'[15]

How is this tyranny exercised? The entire educational system in Ireland, apart from the Christian Brothers' schools, is directly controlled by Great Britain. 'The language of Ireland, the history of Ireland, the economics of Ireland, therefore found no place in their curricula.'[16] Pupils do not know their own country and they judge facts and events according to a point of view that is foreign to them. Primary schools in Ireland act as recruiting sergeants for the British army. At no time is primary education thought of by Griffith as a means for the training and social betterment of the children of the poor, and he contents himself with condemning it as a training ground for soldiers of a foreign country. It is also typical of Griffith's blinkered world-view that he should concentrate his attention on the recruitment of young men – young girls might as well not exist and their education is certainly of no importance to him.

Secondary education is criticised in a completely different way, in a passage which deserves to be quoted in its entirety to show the social viewpoint from which Griffith is writing and which social group he is addressing:

> The secondary system of education in Ireland ... was designed to prevent the higher intelligence of the country performing its duty to the Irish State. In other countries secondary education gives to each its leaders in industry and commerce, its great middle class which as society is constructed forms the equalising and harmonising element in the population. In Ireland secondary education causes aversion and contempt for industry and 'trade' in the heads of young Irishmen, and fixes their eyes, like the fool's, on the ends of the earth. The secondary system in Ireland draws away from industrial pursuits those who are best fitted for them, and sends them to be civil servants in England, or to swell the ranks of struggling clerkdom in Ireland.[17]

This passage is of fundamental importance. The criticism levelled at the primary education is aimed from *without* at the peasant and working-class children who go to these schools; it is a passage dominated by abstractions and its indignation is cold. By contrast, the lines about secondary education tremble with *subjective* indignation. They are aimed at the middle classes frustrated by the colonial status of their country. The term 'employees with no future' corresponds exactly with what must have been felt by the young men from well-to-do families of the time, who every day came up against the obstacles created by the British presence. Arthur Griffith was speaking to the people who were to make up the political forces of the struggle for independence – those who were to become the officers of the IRA and who welcomed the cultural revival as a promise of their own future. Quite naturally they identified their own destiny with that of their country, a destiny in which they could at last play a commanding role.

The solution proposed by Sinn Fein was simple. The Irish people was to take its educational system into its own hands and, with the help of Irish people all over the world and financial contributions from parents, develop a new system of national education. The basis for this education would be the Christian Brothers' schools and, therefore, Roman Catholic. Thanks to the contributions which would flow in from all over the world the schools would be democratic and able to accept rich and poor children alike.

In spite of the pious hope of taking in 'poor children', Griffith was really talking to the middle classes and their offspring. Ireland would be open to them, their prosperity would grow with hers, her interests would be theirs. Civil servants would have to be good nationalists. Irish culture would be the main criterion for recruitment of these new servants of the state:

> In the lowest grades candidates would be required to pass an examination showing an elementary acquaintance with the Irish language, a knowledge of Irish history and an acquaintance with Ireland's resources. In the second grade, the candidate should be required to show himself proficient in Irish history, proficient in the Irish language as a written tongue and proficient in the knowledge of Ireland's resources and possibilities, political and commercial. For the higher grade the candidate should not only possess a full knowledge of the Irish history, but full acquaintance with her early laws and institutions; he should be proficient in Irish both as a written and a spoken language; he should know her literature and understand her art; he should be thoroughly acquainted with Ireland agriculturally, industrially, commercially and topographically; he should know what Ireland has achieved, and be able to show what she could achieve.[18]

It is fascinating to follow the progression of the training of the higher grades in the civil service. The greater the responsibility, the greater the knowledge of the national culture must be. The social function of this knowledge, which had no practical use, was obvious. Having learned a little Irish, lower civil servants would be quite unable to use it as a means of communication at the level where it might become really useful or necessary, for example, in the post-office or town hall. The sole function of this elementary culture was ideological: it was the mark of patriotism and of loyalty to the new state.

At a higher level, a deeper knowledge of the language, especially in its written form, of history, economics and Irish politics was required. But access to the holy of holies of Irish culture was reserved for the highest civil servants. The history of Ireland would not be sufficient; they would also have to understand its origins in Gaelic society and the Brehon laws. Top civil servants must speak and write Irish perfectly, know its literature and understand its art. To sum up, literature, art and mastery of the national language were to be the passport to the highest positions in the state.

This is a decisive passage because it establishes the relationship between the aspirations to independence of young Irish intellectuals, longing to develop their talents and take on the responsibilities which had been denied them, and the literary and cultural revival. The Gaelic circles and impassioned discussion-groups which sprung up across the country can be compared with a vast university at which the Irish nation was in the process of training its political and economic leaders.

Out of this grew a paradox which was the basis of the fundamental misunderstanding between 'poets' and 'politicians'. The literary revival, the cultural nationalism inherited from Thomas Davis, projected into the future the image of a rural simple 'natural' Ireland in which the poets would play the part of spiritual guides. The culture thus passed on was to be the sign of recognition of the new political class which was coming to power and would make Ireland a place where the 'spiritual guides' would have the choice between internal exile, like Sean O'Faolain or emigration, like Sean O'Casey.

Speeches from the Dock

The Sullivan brothers were well-known in nationalist Dublin. A.M. Sullivan was an eminent member of the Irish Party, author of *The Story of Ireland* and organiser of the massive demonstration after the execution of the Manchester Martyrs. He was first a Young Irelander, then succeeded Gavan Duffy as editor and owner of the *Nation*, a journal 'cooler in its Parnellism than the *Freeman's Journal* or *United Ireland*, and ... also more sensitive to ecclesiastical opinion' according to Conor Cruise O'Brien.[19] It published his brother T.D. Sullivan's patriotic poems, such as

'God save Ireland', cried the hero,
God save Ireland, say we all ...

Sung to the tune of 'Tramp, tramp, tramp, the boys are marching', it was used as a nationalist anthem. When the Sullivans published *Speeches from the Dock* in 1890, the book found its way onto every nationalist bookshelf in Dublin. Interviews with nationalist veterans confirmed the success of the book, which was regularly reprinted. From Glasgow, James Connolly sent for copies of *Penny Readings*, containing popular historical material, poems and speeches from the dock.[20]

While Griffith tried to hibernicise the greasy tills of provincial shopkeepers, the Sullivans carefully edited dock speeches in order to prove that Irish patriotism was of an aristocratic brand, untainted by material interests. The biographical sketches of the Irish pantheon gave surprisingly meticulous details about the social status, education and background of the heroes. All of them were men of independent means and good education. They were of course all men, since women must be dependent either as daughters or as wives and so by definition could be neither eloquent nor heroic, except mythically.

Speeches from the Dock was regularly updated and came to span the history of Ireland from the United Irishmen's rebellion to the Anglo-Irish War. Its aim was to refute the charge that Irish rebels were being 'selfish', that is to say fighting for their own interests. In order to rebut this claim, it shows rebels of independent means, whose motives were pure and untainted with political radicalism. As we shall see, Connolly and Larkin, who made dock speeches as good as any, were omitted, no doubt because their patriotism was tainted with socialism and wage-earning. Not so with William Orr, the son of a well-to-do family; his 'comfortable lot and industrious course of life best refute the charge of being an adventurer for plunder'.[21] Henry and John Sheares were affluent lawyers, the sons of a Cork banker. 'On the death of their father, Henry Sheares inherited property yielding an annual income of £1,200 ... Both brothers ... obtained wide practices in their profession, and continued in affluent circumstances up to the day of their arrest.'[22] Such people fight for their country because they love it and are willing to sacrifice their position in life for that love. Wolfe Tone was the grandson of a rich farmer, the son of a successful coachmaker; he 'courted poverty' on account of his commitment.[23] Lord Edward Fitzgerald was 'eloquent and wealthy'.[24] So was Robert Emmet; educated at Trinity College, young, talented, an orator and a poet, he had nothing to do with the 'riotous and noisy rabble' that joined his failed rebellion.[25] Thomas Russell had 'the distinguished marks of a gentleman, a classically moulded head with fine features, and perfect manners'.[26] He did have certain financial difficulties in Belfast, but those were hardly commonplace: 'His generous and trusting nature induced him to go bail for a false friend.'[27] When John Martin undertook medical studies in Trinity, he had 'no idea of earning his living by the profession, but he longed for an opportunity to relieve the suffering of the afflicted poor'.[28] William Smith O'Brien was endowed with nobility, wealth, influence and education. Terence Bellew MacManus was 'young, accomplished, wealthy'; his income was over £1,000 a year, but his patriotism was even greater, 'too genuine to be merged in his commercial success, and MacManus abandoned his prospects and his position as soon as his country seemed to need the sacrifice'.[29] John Mahony was descended from a landowning family, and his patriotism could be called an inherited characteristic.[30] The 'fine hands' of Thomas Clarke Luby were destroyed by oakum picking.[31] John O'Leary was born into a family 'whose circumstances were comfortable and who left to him property that provided him with an annual income of a couple of hundred pounds'.[32]

To sum up, a good patriot is typically a wealthy landlord, or successful professional man, of fine breed and good education, ready to sacrifice his income for the cause and able to make a good speech. What of those whose patriotism was influenced with foreign ideas and did not conform to this pattern? Henry Joy McCracken has no right to a final speech in the Sullivan's anthology, and nor are his origins mentioned either. Could this be because he was too clearly attracted by the alien ideas of the French Revolution?[33] The martyrs of the Easter Rising are all poets or soldiers. James Connolly is described as an 'accomplished writer', but no speech of his is quoted, no mention made of his socialist activities. There is no mention of Larkin, eloquent if not wealthy, nor of Countess Markievicz, who was both eloquent and wealthy, but a woman. In the same way, Michael Davitt dismissed Parnell as an 'unemotional speaker, who never quoted an Irish poet but once, and did it wrong, in a country remarkable for passion and ornate oratory'.[34]

For those whose social status was not in keeping with eloquent patriotism, the Sullivans' lack of enthusiasm is patently obvious. The Fenian leader James Stephens was the son of a clerk, and himself worked as a railway engineer, in contrast with Michael O'Brien who was poor but of whom the Sullivans nevertheless wrote that 'none presented a finer appearance'.[35] The poor, however, did not have the inherited patriotism and eloquence of the wealthy and so were unable to give 'some expression of their patriotism' in front of their judge.[36] The Fenian Bryan Dillon is lacking in eloquence. John Kennedy,

another Fenian and a commercial traveller, had nothing
to say from the dock. Allen, one of the Manchester
Martyrs, was apprenticed with a carpenter; no speech of
his is recorded. It might be argued that uneducated
working-class people really were unable to deliver
flamboyant orations and that the Sullivans could not
invent that which did not exist, but Larkin's absence
from the list is enough to answer this objection. The poor
fellows who did not inherit patriotism with an income
have to prove that they are true patriots. Bryan Dillon
claimed: 'It does not follow because of my social station
that I intended to seize the property of others.'[37]

Logically enough, the social status of traitors and
informers is low. The list of arch-traitor Francis
Higgins's activities is a lengthy one:

> errand-boy, bootblack, porter, hackney-clerk, pervert,
> forger, adventurer, brothel-keeper, informer, betrayer of
> women, invader of domestic happiness, tea-smuggler,
> alleged Irish industrialist, president of the Guild of
> Hosiers ... proprietor of the *Freeman's Journal*, venal
> instrument of the successive Viceroys, general felon-
> setter for the British government.[38]

The poorest of the heroes never sank as low as the
station of an errand-boy, and a role as lowly as that is a
necessary prelude for someone to become a 'betrayer of
women' and a 'felon-setter'.

Speeches from the Dock is more a popular history of
Ireland than a collection of speeches. It is a 'people's
history' of nationalist and Catholic Ireland from which
the people are excluded. John Martin is explicit about
this: his aim was to establish the national independence
of Ireland 'for the benefit of all the people of Ireland –
noblemen, clergymen, judges, professional men – in fact
all Irishmen'.[39] Farmers, workers and industrialists are
not Irishmen. Land wars, social struggles and strikes are
not part of the heroic saga. The social upheavals of
Belfast in 1907 and Dublin in 1913 are omitted. Irishmen
'occupied with commercial and professional pursuits,

were less energetic than the members of the Fenian brotherhood in their political action'.[40]

It must be remembered that the main charge against Fenianism was that it was influenced by socialist and other foreign revolutionary ideas. The accused were keen to answer this charge by saying that their motives were pure and their patriotism untainted by class hatred. The Fenians were 'pledged by word of honour to promote love and harmony amongst all classes of Irishmen'. There was no question of seizing the property of others. 'Revolutionists are not ruffians or raparees.' In this respect, the best representatives of disinterested patriotism were the Irish-Americans because they had no material stake at all in the country. 'My motives were pure, patriotic, unselfish,' said Captain William McKay.[41] In fact, they have sacrificed everything for their country.

Conversely, the English invaders use material interest to 'bribe' Irishmen into servility. Sir John Maxwell, commander in chief of British forces in Ireland, demanded that the bishops take sanctions against the priests who showed sympathy for the rebels of 1916. Dr O'Dwyer, Bishop of Limerick, answered proudly enough to be quoted in *Speeches from the Dock*, exposing the alien rulers, Gladstone as 'some English barrister from Bristol', and Disraeli as 'some Jew from Shoreditch', who 'buy the national Press ... demoralise individuals, and even, large classes, by an insidious system of bribery'.[42] Who on earth could these 'large classes' of Irishmen be, bribed by the English? Could they be the Protestant workers of the North, alienated from true patriotism, and from the true faith as well, by higher wages? In other words, could there be some logic in the fact that the 'true patriots' are members of the upper classes? Being rich, they are much less susceptible to bribery.

Eloquent but not so Wealthy

The Clanking of Chains by Brinsley MacNamara, author of *The Valley of the Squinting Windows*, takes place in the small town of Ballycullen in the years preceding the Anglo-Irish War. The hero of the novel, Michael Dempsey, a shop-assistant, tries to share his nationalist enthusiasm with the local community. The novel ends with his predictable failure and exile since it starts with the quote:

Romantic Ireland's dead and gone
It's with O'Leary in the grave.

Ballycullen is clearly divided into two camps: on the one hand, Michael Dempsey, the hero, and two of his friends who can only triumph and revel in failure: Kevin Shanaghan, a ruined drunkard, who had been a peasant leader during the Land War, and Connor Carberry, an ex-Fenian and convict in Australia. On the other side are the rest of the people, farmers, shop-keepers, businessmen, cattle-merchants. Michael Dempsey is aflame with nationalist dreams, a great reader of patriotic poems and histories of Ireland. The others are only preoccupied with their 'greasy tills'.

Michael is rehearsing a play called *Robert Emmet*. The rehearsal takes place in a bank overpowered by the stink of money. When the young men and women of the theatrical troupe come into the hall, 'life', that is to say art, joy and purity, takes the place of the stench of mammon. Michael is the last person to arrive at the rehearsal. He is the charismatic leader, his face is shining with an inner light, and everybody turns round to look at him on his arrival. On the third page, he is still the only character to have a name. His part in the play is that of Robert Emmet, of course, while the girl whom he secretly loves plays the role of Sarah Curran. The hierarchy of values is clearly depicted. On top, Michael Dempsey is leader, chief and Messiah. He is the only one who is well-read. In the Sinn Fein programme, he would be placed at the pinnacle of the civil service elite. For the Sullivans, he would be an impoverished hero, but endowed with eloquence. The others have no name, they

stutter clumsily through their parts, though their faults
are redeemed by a yearning for 'life'.

This presentation is based on an implicit conception of
art as life. Art is life. To play is to act. Great art is the
story of a great life. Quite logically, the part of the traitor
is played by Ambrose Donohoe, a 'shoneen', a subscriber
to filthy English weeklies. This naïve conception is
shared by the audience. When the play is performed on
the eve of the First World War, Dempsey-Emmet is
frantically cheered by the audience: 'It was the most
awful orgy of patriotism ever seen in Ballycullen ... They
cheered Michael as if he were ... some new and inspired
saviour of Ireland.'[43] The actor becomes the political
leader. Exhilarated by the applause, Michael, after the
curtain has gone down and the magic of the show is gone,
steps forward and delivers a straightforward political
speech demanding the establishment of a 'Republic of
Ireland'. But by now, he has become a shop-assistant
again and the people shout him down, thinking he is
drunk – which he is, drunk with words, sound and fury.

From the fateful day when Michael Dempsey accepted
the part of Robert Emmet, he was doomed to failure.
Emmet's words became his own, he is transfigured, art
has lifted him to summit where he is alone, aloof from the
crowd. The performance was an initiation rite, the
gateway to martyrdom. Henceforth, Michael will walk
the Way of the Cross in the streets of Ballycullen, beaten
and insulted by the small town which is the epitome of
Ireland, a corpse on the dissecting table. He is a member
of the elite whose suffering is the necessary sacrifice for
the redemption of the people.

Michael Dempsey is a literary Fenian. It has already
been argued that Fenianism was a history of bungled
insurrections, spectacular failures redeemed by flamboyant speeches. Dempsey is isolated in Ballycullen, but he
is right and Ballycullen is wrong. The town is inhabited
by people who are unable to understand they have a
country. There is no spark of rebellion left. The only
glimmer of patriotism is the idea that the greatness of

the country can be the sum total of individual success. The real patriots are consequently those who have a material stake in the country. Crude examples of this self-interest are given in the novel. When the Irish Volunteers start their military training, the shoneen Ambrose Donohoe makes a quick profit by selling the wooden guns. In 1918, during the rise of Sinn Fein, the shopkeeper Seumas MacEvoy launches a successful trade in patriotic paraphernalia, books, newspapers, song-sheets and badges. Such attitudes run directly counter the general philosophy of *Speeches from the Dock*: heroes never act out of self-interest. Personal success is a great destroyer of patriotism. 'They got the land – so what do they care now about the noble cry of Nationality?' complains the old Fenian leader.[44] No wonder the people of Ballycullen support John Redmond instead of the Fenians, consider the Dublin strikers of 1913 as an unruly mob and Larkin as a rabble-rouser. The shop-keepers are horrified by the plunder of goods during the Easter Rising.

Confronted with such apathy, Michael is alone and revels in his isolation. In fact, his greatest fear is that Ballycullen should share his commitment. His suffering is not a failure, and loneliness proves that he is on the right road. Given the state of the people, success would mean either that the hero descend to the general level of opinion, which is unthinkable, or that the crowd should rise to the summit of the prophet, which is impossible. His mood remains the same when the town shows its support for Sinn Fein in 1918 because Sinn Fein is no longer the small, elect organisation for dreamers and prophets:

> The truth, in the nature of a triumph to a great many, but to him and a few others as something more nearly akin to defeat, was that Sinn Fein had become a political party ... The election of Count Plunkett for North Roscommon was made to appear an event of more real and actual importance to the New Ireland than the Rebellion of Easter Week.[45]

The defeat of 1916 is a victory, the success of 1918 is a defeat. So the greatest danger is success. How does one avoid being successful? By hiding one's ideas as thoroughly as possible. 'He knew the joy of pondering his thoughts in unsullied loneliness, for there comes a great kindliness from the unspoken thought.'[46] During long sleepless nights, he draws the maps and particulars of a plan of insurrection. 'This was a better plan than Robert Emmet's.'[47] Was it a better plan because fewer people were acquainted with it? 'It was almost a thing of ecstasy, this hidden heroism.'[48] He writes a letter to the press, but does not send it. Salvation can only come by a 'miracle of God' through chosen people. Why not Michael Dempsey himself? 'All down the ages there had been manifestations of the Holy Spirit through such lowly people as he was.'[49] The miracle of God had taken place: it was the performance of the play that transformed a menial shop-assistant into a prophet.

In *The Clanking of Chains* the way in which cultural nationalism could influence budding intellectuals is clearly depicted. Influenced by the tradition of the Young Irelanders, the Fenians and national poetry, they saw themselves as potential prophets for their country. More than a political leader, Michael Dempsey is a poet rejected by the ignorant crowd. He does not like the world around him, so he transforms it into a work of art. Sinn Fein was originally a fine organisation because it refused 'the disturbing element of political development'. At that stage, the rebellion it was preparing would bring about the millenium 'in one great crash of poetic justice'.[50] Men like Michael Dempsey were perfectly at ease in what Ernie O'Malley called 'the lyrical stage' in *On Another Man's Wounds*. When the future is uncertain, the poet thinks he can shape the world as he shapes his poems. But after the lyrical stage comes the hard work of organisation, compaigning and elections. Before then, there was a short, blissful period in which Ireland was a country where the marriage of the poetic dream and social reality seemed possible.

Sinn Fein ... had managed successfully to adjust itself to the moment, because, by a political coincidence, the moment itself was in the melodramatic tradition of the past. It might not be able to adjust itself to the new political development which must arise inevitably out of the economic realities of peace conditions with their certain monstrous aspects of surprise.[51]

Notes

1   Sean O'Faolain, 'The Stuffed Shirts', *Bell*, June 1943.
2   *The Ethics of Sinn Fein*, Dublin 1917, p. 5.
3   Ibid., p. 1.
4   Ibid., p. 2.
5   Ibid., p. 3.
6   Ibid., p. 7.
7   Ibid., p. 0.
8   Ibid., p. 5.
9   Mary Hayden, *Facts About the Irish Language and the Irish Language Movements*, Dublin 1910. This pamphlet was published by the Gaelic League 'for the information of the members of the Irish Home-Going Association and other visitors'.
10   Ibid., p. 14.
11   Ibid., p. 15.
12   Ibid., p. 15–6.
13   James Connolly, *Workers' Republic*, 1 October 1898, reprinted in *Socialism and Nationalism*, Dublin 1948.
14   *The Ethics of Sinn Fein*, p. 5.
15   Ibid., p. 8.
16   Ibid., p. 5.
17   Ibid., p. 23.
18   Ibid.
19   Conor Cruise O'Brien, *Parnell and His Party*, Oxford 1968, p. 306.
20   C. Desmond Greaves, *The Life and Times of James Connolly*, London 1972, p. 26.
21   A.M. and T.D. Sullivan (eds), *Speeches from the Dock*, Dublin 1968, p. 6.
22   Ibid., p. 25.
23   Ibid.
24   Ibid., p. 28.
25   Ibid., p. 35.
26   Ibid., p. 46.
27   Ibid.
28   Ibid., p. 73.
29   Ibid., p. 118.
30   Ibid., p. 30.
31   Ibid., p. 137.
32   Ibid., p. 138.
33   Thomas Pakenham, *The Year of Liberty*, London 1969, p. 416.

34   Michael Davitt, *The Fall of Feudalism in Ireland or the Story of the Land League Revolution*, New York 1904, p. 652.
35   A.M. and T.D. Sullivan (eds), op. cit., p. 243.
36   Ibid., p. 147.
37   Ibid., p. 148.
38   Ibid., p. 320.
39   Ibid., p. 80.
40   Ibid., p. 205.
41   Ibid., p. 200.
42   Ibid., p. 317.
43   Brinsley MacNamara, *The Clanking of Chains*, Tralee 1965, p. 94.
44   Ibid., p. 49.
45   Ibid., pp. 129–30.
46   Ibid., p. 69.
47   Ibid., p. 98.
48   Ibid., p. 39.
49   Ibid., p. 98.
50   Ibid., p. 133.
51   Ibid.

3 On the Land

We want to see as many people as possible on the land.
                                        Eamon De Valera[1]

The revivalists sought in Ireland the kind of dignity and
the kind of health that the industrialised world, the
modern world had lost; the Ireland they loved had an
enormous West Coast and no North-East corner.
                                        Conor Cruise O'Brien[2]

At the end of the nineteenth century Ireland was at a
crossroads. Independence was within reach and every
cultural or political organisation working for independence had its own vision of the country's future. For
some, industrial development was a necessary condition
for real independence. They saw their country's future as
a 'Gaelic Manchester', with the 'Gaelic' tag very much in
second place. Others refused to accept the industrial
model and imagined Ireland as one vast pasture in which
cultured shepherds periodically gathered together to
recite verses and sing time-honoured songs. Sinn Fein
and the workers' movement chose the industrialisation
card. The Gaelic League, the partisans of the cultural
revival and, above all, the writers of the literary revival,
absolutely refused to accept the English model of
development. Sean O'Casey wrote in the *Irish Worker* in
1913: 'Ireland never was, never will be ... furnace-burned
... Commercialism was far from her shores ... she, in her
language, national dramatic revival, has turned her back
upon Mammon.'[3]
The creator of the master-images of this mythology
was Yeats. His *Autobiographies* reveal, as much in his

formative years as in the memories he cherished later, an entirely rural Ireland. The people who populated his memories were essentially peasants or servants, endlessly telling stories about the exploits of fairies, goblins and elves. When Yeats started to write, he remembered Sligo with 'tears in his eyes'. That is where he wanted to find an audience.[4] It was in the countryside that one could find the true, the living language – that of both peasants and aristocrats. As we have seen, the two groups were closely linked, since the peasants of the legend were aristocrats fallen on hard times, the descendants of kings and bards. He named them 'Knights of the Sheep',[5] telling stories 'that Homer might have told'.[6] Peasant communities are the custodians of human culture and its enduring principles, whilst urban culture is artificial and fleeting.

> Folk-art is, indeed, the oldest of the aristocracies of thought and because it refuses what is passing and trivial, the merely clever and pretty as certainly as the vulgar and the insincere, and because it has gathered into itself the simplest and most unforgettable thoughts of the generations, it is the soil where all great art is rooted.[7]

Here one sees the 'Knight of the Sheep' at work with the double definition of folklore as the nobility of ideas and the soil in which art is rooted. Soil, land, fields – Yeats never forgot them. In London he longed to have a lump of soil in his hand, a piece of the Sligo he knew.[8] This had nothing to do with the peasant's love for the earth he crumbles in his fingers, even if Yeats plays with the double meaning of the term 'peasant culture'. The value of peasant culture is to be seen in the opposition of town and country. In the *Irish Worker* article mentioned above O'Casey based his argument on the opposition of the two concepts. Ireland was characterised by her language, literature, theatre, earth, trees and her happy people, Britain by her textiles, glass, blast-furnaces, commercialism, old age pensions, social security and meals for needy children. The opposition is between town and country, or between 'soul' and materialism. For O'Casey in 1913, the Irish had a soul and the English had none, in the same way as Yeats had said the Irish 'had not been corrupted by commercialism'. Not surprisingly, this is also the standard position of the Catholic church, which considered the country to be uncorrupted by foreign influences. During the Second World War the church considered Britain's Beveridge Plan, which paved the way for the Welfare State, as 'not for export. It is rather an incentive to avoid those conditions that make such plans inevitable.'[9]

The same themes were developed at length in Yeats's *Celtic Twilight*, a collection of Irish legends.[10] *Kidnappers* tells the story of a woman who disappeared one fine day from the garden where she had been working with her husband. Later, her son found out that she was being kept prisoner in Glasgow. He went there and found his mother working in a cellar:

> She was happy, she said, and had the best of good eating, and would he not eat? ... but, he knowing well that she was trying to cast on him the glamour by giving him faery food ... refused and came home to his people in Sligo.[11]

The town is Hell, and the mother lives below ground. The town is abroad and represents emigration. The town means unhealthy work. Food is an important element in this mythology and the spell of evil food represents the town-dwellers' dangerous food. Town-dwellers may benefit from old age pensions, social security and meals for needy children, but the price they have to pay for this is physical ruin and the loss of their souls. Peter O'Leary explained in *My Story* how people were losing their teeth because they had given up milk and potatoes for tea and meat. This same evil food is eating away the faces of people living in London:

> Certain old women's faces filled me with horror ... fat blotched faces rising above double chins, or women who have drunk too much beer and eaten much meat. In Dublin I had often seen old women walking with erect

heads and gaunt bodies, talking to themselves with loud
voices, mad with drink and poverty, but they were
different, they belonged to romance.[12]

Since then we have learned to be chary of the romance of
poverty, but in the early twentieth century this sort of
attitude to poverty was widespread both in Ireland and
elsewhere. Yeats's use of this expression is aristocratic
and reveals the distance between the two streams of the
literary renaissance. A certain number of people,
particularly members of the Gaelic League, tried to
rediscover the Ireland hidden under the relatively new
varnish of English culture and language. They tried to
express the oral culture which belonged to these
communities and succeeded in producing works in Irish,
particularly autobiographies. In the stories that were
collected in this way people do not joke about the
marvellous aspects of poverty. 'We are poor, simple
people, living from hand-to-mouth. I fancy we should
have been no better off if we had been misers,' says Tomas
O Crohan.[13] Peig Sayers's sentiments are no less clear
when she finds out that the government is going to give
her a pension. All the widows in the village were excited
at the prospect and waited anxiously.[14] The attitude of
Yeats, Lady Gregory, and, to a lesser degree, Synge was
entirely different. They did not want or try to modernise
a culture, they simply showed that they were able to feel
in harmony with the peasant world and its culture. The
sieve of their sensitivity retained only the purest gold of
the Gaelic past. Misery was never poverty for them but
was turned into rich tapestries. The egotistic character of
their interest in the Irish peasant is striking. It is not a
dialogue, a mutual enriching: they *took*, but they gave
back nothing: 'I did not examine ... the true thoughts of
those I met, nor the general condition of the country, but
I examined myself a great deal.'[15] When reading Yeats's
comments on the happiness of these simple folk, the
French anthropologist Michel Leiris's observation
immediately springs to mind: 'One is only inclined to

regard as happy a people who make *us* happy because of the poetical or aesthetic emotion which the sight of them inspires in us.'[16]

Lest these remarks be considered harsh, a word of explanation is possibly necessary at this point. A meeting between a literary movement and the peasant way of life is not a new phenomenon. The romantic reaction to industry and towns is well-known. Romantic nationalism dates back to early nineteenth-century Germany. It considered the people as an organic whole, with fundamental expressions: language, manners, myths considered not as superstitions but as a feature of the national character, as *Volksdichtung* (folk science). Hegel first wrote of the concept of *Volkgeist* (the spirit of the people) in 1793 and Arndt that of *Volkseele* (the soul of the people) in 1806. Whereas the upper layers of society are corrupted by cosmopolitism, the culture of the people is strong and ancient. The people is the mother of history. It was this culture that inspired the patriots and the nationalists and their hope for liberation from the foreign yoke. In 1858, Riehl created the expression *Volkskunde* (science of the people) which studied the origin, the language, customs and housing of the people. 'The people' was aesthetically revalued: its oral literature was naïve and fresh, with a colourful and dense language, its music original and spontaneous. Its ethics were revalued: traditional sayings were considered as wise. The people represented the pure and the authentic against the impure and adulterated.

Yeats and his literary friends were obviously caught in the same line of ideas, but what concerns us here is not Yeats's poetical work but the success of a myth to which he contributed through his literary work. It is a fact that in spite of the gulf between this myth and social reality, it was taken seriously, survived and contributed to the shaping of the mentality of the Irish people. The myth of a rural civilisation did not only dominate the literary renaissance, it also overshadowed the country's religious and political life. Like nationalism, it played a unifying role by giving a common vocabulary to Irishmen who were deeply divided on other matters. 'The ignorant peasants are the most interesting portion of the population,' wrote D.P. Moran in 1905. 'The farmers are the most stable human element in the life of a nation,' wrote George Russell, who thought that primitive social virtues developed better in the countryside than in the towns.[17] Michael Collins, a military leader in the Anglo-Irish war, repeated the same sentiments:

> Impoverished as the people are ... the outward aspect is a pageant. One may see processions of young women riding down on Island ponies to collect sand from the seashore or gathering turf, dressed in their shawls and in their brilliantly coloured skirts made of material spun, woven and dyed by themselves ... Their cottages also are little changed. They remain simple and picturesque. It is only in such places that one gets a glimpse of what Ireland may become again.[18]

It would be difficult to find people as different in personality and opinions as D.P. Moran, George Russell and Michael Collins, but in spite of their differences they were on common ground on this issue and spoke the same language. This is not surprising. The nature of this myth is vague enough and rich enough to stand contradictory interpretations.

We have already noted that the Anglo-Irish writers were opposed to industrialisation. Synge was afraid of the destructive progress of commerce and reform in the Aran Islands. Like Yeats and George Russell, he was conscious of the conflict between material security and the riches of the imagination, conscious too of the link between popular culture and the dangers of life on the land and at sea. However, their 'choice' was foreign to Irish reality. On those few occasions when peasant communities had the chance to choose between imagination and material security, they never hesitated in opting for the latter. The criticism levelled at the writers of the literary revival by Sinn Fein and the Roman Catholic church, that they had come to rob Gaelic culture in order to enrich a culture foreign to the Irish people, was not without foundation. These writers were in harmony not with the peasant world but with an image of it. Their harking back to the past was imported from Europe and directly linked with the medieval romanticism of English writers like William Morris.

The gap between the literary images and the way the people felt about themselves becomes very clear on re-reading the 'Irish' autobiographies, like *Twenty Years A-Growing* and *The Islandman*. The world of these peasants and fishermen was made up of close-knit, isolated communities which evolved very slowly. These men and women were not masters of their environment – they were completely subject to it. They feared foreign influence. The unknown was by definition hostile. Natural phenomena such as storms, bad weather and poor harvests were neither more nor less explicable than famine, emigration, eviction, war and uprisings. Their range of experience was narrow and limited. The first time the Blasket Islanders saw a steamship they thought the boat was on fire. The first time they saw a black man it had to be explained to them that he had been born that way. The first time they saw a man with glasses the schoolchildren shouted 'that the man came from Hell'. Either in blessed ignorance or resignation, catastrophes came and went, caused by unknown powers, the result of fate:

> The very first of them that we christened was only seven or eight years old when he fell over the cliff and was killed. From that time on they went as quickly as they came. Two died of measles, and every epidemic that came carried off one or other of them ... All these things were a sore trouble to the poor mother, and she, too, was taken from me ... Such was the fate of my children. May God's blessing be with them.[19]

There was no interest in foreign affairs, and 'abroad' began close at hand. War or revolutions were only understood in so far as they affected daily life. In *Twenty Years A-Growing*, a character asks why war is a bad thing. The reply is simple: 'Who will buy the fish from us, who will buy the pig or the cow?'[20] The wrecking of a ship off the coast was a blessing for the poor Blasket Islanders: 'Those were bad years, and if it hadn't been for that shipwreck, nobody would have survived.' The whole crew was drowned, but its cargo saved the inhabitants from starvation: 'It was God who sent her to the poor.'[21] War was sometimes therefore seen as a blessing for the poor because it sends wrecks with their tins of food and sacks of flour. 'Lord God! What a marvellous sight ... we were jumping for joy.'[22] As George Russell said, primitive social virtues do better in the country than in the town.

This resignation in the face of destiny is sometimes broken by sudden eruptions of violence. These explosions are not out of context with daily life; on the contrary, they express the violence of individual and social relationships. Hurling matches were, more often than not, demonstrations of brute force. Fishermen fought for the spoils from wrecks or shoals of fish, and often went home bloodied and bruised. Sometimes, however, this violence was directed against other targets whilst retaining its characteristic, sudden, feverish onset. Rebellion never got past the stage of sudden revolt. Tax-collectors were thrown back into the sea by fishermen's wives chasing after them with stones.[23]

Is there any injustice or sacrilege in not finding any trace of the rich life of village communities in these peasant memoirs? Their material life was poor and their cultural life was constrained by a language which isolated them all the more and formed a screen separating them from the outside world. What is striking about these autobiographies is that these people's culture is only expressed when they come into contact with outsiders. Their experience is enriched when it comes into contact with other experiences. 'It's amazing what a lot there is in an old man's head when *someone else* starts him talking and puts questions to him.'[24]

Brian O'Kelly encouraged Tomas O Crohan to write his book by giving him Gorky's autobiography, *My*

Childhood, the same book that Maurice O'Sullivan read
before setting out to tell the story of his life.[25] One of the
aims of the Irish cultural renaissance was to 'make the
peasants speak' in the Irish language.

It is not difficult to show the distance between the ideal
peasant of the literary revival and the less than ideal
peasants who actually lived in the Gaelic-speaking West.
What may be of greater interest is to understand how the
poets took the road to the country. Like poets, academics
were attracted by the West of Ireland. The anthropologist
Hugh Brody went West after reading Maurice O'Sullivan's *Twenty Years A-Growing.* On his first visit in 1966,
he was received by a sixty-year-old woman, Kate Ness:

> Kate showed how beautifully she could lilt a Gaelic air ...
> pushed aside her kitchen furniture to make room for a jig,
> or sat on the seat at the edge of a turf fire to tell long
> stories of her life in the country and of its people, or
> showed the best music while milking a troubled cow.[26]

But he described the process which D.P. Moran feared
most: contact with the outside world, modernisation and
emigration are all powerful factors in the destruction of a
traditional way of life. Young people do not find work.
They emigrate and send home letters which justify their
decision. In spite of this, according to Brody, until the
1920s those who stayed behind maintained a certain
trust in their future as farmers, in their way of life. What
really destroyed 'Inishkillane' was the achievement of
material autonomy through the Wyndham Acts and
political independence. Against 'foreign landlords' and
foreign oppression, the rural world was fighting in the
name of values the farmers really believed in. When they
became real farmers – independent, owner-occupiers of
their land – their world and their values crumbled. Only
poets and academics live on mythology. For the son
waiting to inherit the farm, the price to pay is a long
drawn-out engagement. If he does not inherit the farm,
buying or renting land is often impossible. A career in the
church is accessible only to those who do well at school.

The only alternative is emigration. The process is irresistible:

> The process of criticism and comparison, the development
> of consciousness in those socially best placed for criticism
> and most burdened by the formerly accepted system is not
> easily halted once it is under way.[27]

Meanwhile, the literati were fascinated by the living presence of legends, stories and poems in these communities. The peasants and fishermen believed in fairies, ghosts and goblins not as external powers but as invisible presences and active witnesses of a society of which they were full members. The visible and invisible worlds were not separated by an impenetrable frontier. Passages from one world to the other were frequent, both in time and space, and had an effect on all aspects of human activity.[28] People really saw those who had emigrated to America back in their own gardens, or dead people chatting on their doorsteps. In such an environment, legends, stories and oral poetry were manifestations of everyday magic. The story-teller was a magician and the stories and characters he invented were as real as the dead people come back to the village. He made people laugh and cry with words, and when he frightened them all eyes turned towards the window to watch out for the ghost. To writers whose work was the creation of fictional worlds, the potency of the story-teller's language, the respect and power it enjoyed, must have both fascinating and attractive. In the rural society of the West of Ireland they could see their ideal alive, the image of the Ireland they wanted to fashion, a rural society directed by a new aristocracy, the aristocracy of the mind. This model of society was rooted in the images handed down in the history of the country. For George Russell the Gaelic clan was aristocratic in its government and democratic in its social structure. The leaders were democratic in their economic theory and had that freedom of spirit proper to the aristocracy.[29]

The writers felt that the masses had lost their leaders

and were 'looking for light', according to D.P. Moran.[30] They were ready to take up the torch. The West was where the new cultural frontiers were, and the new territories to be cultivated. They reckoned on finding a world equivalent to Gaelic society in which the poet was a member of the ruling elite, an alluring prospect at a time when they felt crushed by the implacable wave of 'materialism' elsewhere in Europe.

The poetics of politics was so strong that it was Michael Davitt's principal criticism of Parnell. Davitt recalled that:

> The Land League movement appealed to poetic patriot-ism ... of tuneful propagandists, and few meetings came off in the West or South which had not its singer with some 'lament' of a hero of agrarian repute, or versified malediction upon an evictor or other obnoxious enemy of the cause.[31]

Charles Stewart Parnell obviously did not share the culture and religion of the peasantry. When he spoke on electoral platforms, he employed the reasoning of English philosophers rather than Gaelic lilts and laments. Davitt noted a priest's response at one such meeting: 'This young man comes to Meath and talks a great deal of J.S. Mill, but I'd like to tell him that the priests of Meath know nothing about J.S. Mill.'[32] Nothing more need be said: Parnell's demise was predictable. He was a foreigner, alien to the 'true faith', and lived too much outside the country: 'His immense popularity with the Irish people was not due to any Celtic qualities. Of these he had not even a trace. There is no racial affinity between him and them.'[33] Parnell was cold and reserved, and his major crime has already been mentioned: he never quoted Irish poets, and instead cited English philosophers like John Stuart Mill in his speeches. The 'ornate oratory' thus became a kind of dam against the 'vicious vocabulary of the continent' which, according to Archbishop Croke, was about to swoop down on Ireland.[34]

There is a strange passage about the Gaelic poet
Dunlevy in *The Islandman* in which the narrator, Tomas,
wants to spend the day bringing in turf but meets
Dunlevy on the way and cannot refuse to listen to him or
to take down his poems in writing, 'for fear he would turn
the rough side of his tongue to me'. Tomas therefore loses
a day's work, complains about this wasted time and
thinks, 'I fancy that no poet has ever been much good at
carrying through any job that had any work in it except
only poetry.'[35] This scene is an exact picture – almost a
re-enactment – of the poem already quoted praising the
poet's life. This picture of a traditional poet, able through
the power of his words alone to keep a peasant from his
work, must have had a profound effect on the
Dublin-based poets.

The reason why the myth of a rural civilisation does
not disappear with the rural ways of life is quite simple.
Born outside the country, it had a certain resonance in
Ireland, but had no more social basis in the nineteenth
century than it did after independence. It could thus
happily live on precisely because of its lack of roots.

Rural Intellectuals: The Priests

If by 'intellectuals' one designates a group of people
whose training, education and accumulation of knowledge allow them to express the ideological system of a
community in a coherent fashion, then the most
important intellectuals in the Irish countryside were
without doubt the priests rather than primary-school
teachers.

The social standing of the priests drew them nearer to
the 'fili' than to the village teachers. For the Roman
Catholic peasantry the only hope of a rise in social status
for male children was to make priests of them. 'When it
was obvious that I would never make a priest the sole
ambition of my mother was that I become a shop-
assistant,' remembered Frank O'Connor.[36] In his
autobiography, Canon Peter O'Leary explains that from

a very young age he wanted to become a priest but that no one took him seriously because he came from a family that was too poor to pay for his studies.[37] Even if priests from a poor rural background did not rise very high in the ecclesiastical hierarchy, the priesthood was still considered as highly prestigious.

Most novels set in the Irish countryside mention the status of the priest in the rural community. In *The Valley of the Squinting Windows*, the main character in the village is Father O'Keefe, whose authority is never questioned.[38] Two other characters are students, future members of the elite, one a medical student, the other, John Brennan, a future priest. The novel is held together from start to finish by the anxious waiting of John's mother, for whom her son's entry into the priesthood will be the crowning glory of a life of effort and self-sacrifice.

In the context of a rural community, the priest played the role of the 'intellectual' as a result of his cultural and political influence, much more than any other member of the community. Like 'the poet', he was attached to the broader currents of European thought, to a church whose centre was outside the country. He was subject to a type of loyalty different to that of the political or cultural activists. He was a member of an institution whose terms of reference were different, which operated according to its own laws, sometimes in accordance with national aspirations, sometimes cut off from them, but at all times attached by intimate links to the mass of the people. The priest was, therefore, torn between opposing loyalties which he tried to reconcile. In a more natural way than the urban intellectuals, and precisely because he was a child of these country people, he was attached by a thousand ties to the peasant community from which he came.

With its transparent naïvety, Peter O'Leary's auto-biography *My Story* is an excellent window onto the status of the priest in the Irish countryside. Although written by a priest, religion and theology play remarkably little part in the book; there is not a single qualm of conscience or a piece of private anguish in this diary of a country priest. Before being Catholic, religion is national. The autobiography is above all a pretext for giving a personal view of Ireland's destiny and admits to a single-minded obsession with national belonging. When the book was first published in 1915 it was welcomed enthusiastically as the first 'modern' book written in Irish and was subsequently widely used as a textbook for teaching the national language.

In his introduction, C.T. O Ceirin, who translated the book into English, presents the work as a social document. O Ceirin sympathises fully, without any critical distancing, with the spirit which imbues the book, which is decribed as 'infused with the spirit of the emerging nation'; it is above criticism in the same way as the poems in the *Nation*, which form a 'historical memorial'. He draws the conclusion that men such as O'Leary represent a much deeper and more durable tendency in Irish society than do some of the more spectacular movements which grew out of foreign theories uneasily grafted onto the nation's history:

> Despite what the history books may say, the influence of a Wolfe Tone or a Robert Emmet, of the French Revolution or any other -isms was only skin deep in this people. When Canon O'Leary thinks of insurrection, theories do not enter in it ...[39]

The idea that 'isms' are not Irish is well-rooted in nationalist literature from Mitchel in his *Jail Journal* to Griffith and, as we shall see, Father Shaw writing on Pearse.

The true Irish people were not Wolfe Tone and Robert Emmett, nor even Grattan and Thomas Davis. The true inheritors of the tradition of Daniel O'Connell and Michael Davitt were, rather, men such as Peter O'Leary. The tradition of O'Connell and Davitt, as opposed to that of Wolfe Tone's United Irishmen, was truly national and benefited from truly popular support: the great mass of the populace followed Daniel O'Connell and Michael

Davitt led 'the indomitable Ireland'.[40] The two names quoted are, of course, those of Roman Catholics, rather than the Protestants Tone, Grattan, Emmett and Davis.

Peter O'Leary begins with a brief history of Ireland, a traditional nationalist history which may be paraphrased thus: the Irish people fought against the enemy for the cause of their country and faith. Nationalism and Roman Catholicism are one and the same. English oppression is reduced to its religious aspects. The ancestors were dispossessed of their land 'when they would not deny their faith'.[41] O'Leary's most important roots were thus both historical and national. The accent is then put on his peasant origins. He did not come from the outside to bring the good news, but was a member of the community whom destiny had chosen as the most suitable and articulate to give a voice to its culture and aspirations. Son and grandson of peasants, he faithfully expressed the slowness to change, the fear of innovation, the mistrust of everything which came from the town. The new generation, he wrote, is a lot less strong than his own. Why? Because of 'modern' food:

> If people would only throw away the tea and the white loaf and start taking potatoes and milk as their food and drink again ... they'd have teeth and stomachs and health every bit as good as their fathers had.[42]

Potatoes and milk as against tea and white bread. This was how the two civilisations, the two ways of life, were opposed to each other. Potatoes and milk are Ireland against England, country versus town, agriculture versus industry. Without reading too much into the text, one could almost add to the list the good milk of Roman Catholicism as opposed to the adulterated tea of Protestantism ...

This opposition between the peasant world and the town is very deep. The urban world is far away, hostile and foreign. The only familiar landscape is that of the village, at once a religious and a cultural community. The only struggles which involve the people are issues affecting the peasantry. The town almost never appears in *My Story*. Any walls which are higher than those of the cloister have a disturbing character and are as constraining as prison walls. O'Leary therefore presents his time at the seminary in Maynooth as a break difficult to bear before the longed-for return to the village. In the chapter devoted to Maynooth, O'Leary gives no hint as to the content of his studies, the training of young priests or the relationship between students and their teachers. He constantly underlines the disastrous consequences of college life on the health of the future priests. Their frequent illnesses are due, according to him, to the effect of high walls on students used to wide-open spaces and to the 'foreign food' – meat instead of potatoes and rye bread. Peter O'Leary compares Maynooth unfavourably with the traditional educational system of Gaelic society:

> Neither teacher nor students had any fine, big slated houses ... everybody has his own small house – nice and well-sheltered with a good thatched roof on it, and no furniture in it except for a table and a bed and a couple of chairs, perhaps, and the hearth. We are told that it was normal for the students to be going round about the neighbourhood 'gathering' milk for themselves. They hadn't got the grand walls round them like we had, but I reckon that their health was better than that of the Maynooth College.[43]

O'Leary's memoirs cover the period from the Famine to the First World War. His career was typical of that of a priest attached to the national cause; he was opposed to the Fenian movement, became actively involved both in the Land League and the Gaelic League and supported Sinn Fein to the end of his days. In spite of the absence of the explicit political references, his choices are quite clearly stated from the very first chapter, 'My Ancestors'. Ranged on one side are 'my people', the Roman Catholic people of Ireland who are fighting the 'foreigners' – the enemy, the plunderers and robbers. All these terms are as clear as day to the reader even though the words 'English' or 'Protestant' are never used. Although deeply rooted in his own area, not one of the eddies of the nation's life leaves him indifferent. The accusation to which he is most sensitive is that which denies his church its national character. *My Story* is a political book from beginning to end, the object of which is to prove by means of a personal example that Irish Roman Catholics are good patriots.

Viewed from this perspective, the most painful episode was the Roman Catholic church's opposition to, and condemnation of, the Fenian movement. The reasons given for this condemnation were the Fenians' aims and methods. The Fenian movement, it was claimed, was infiltrated by subversive and anti-religious theories which came from France. It advocated violence and military action. O'Leary's justification of the church's position does not take up either of these points. The starting point is neither religion nor the role of the church, but the national cause. O'Leary is not hostile to violence as such, indeed, he is sympathetic in his recounting of stories of big-hearted brigands who stole money from the rich and gave it to the poor. For O'Leary, the reasons for the church's condemnation of the Fenians were thoroughly political and pragmatic; they were condemned because their venture was doomed to failure:

> The clergy of Ireland and the old people had a long acquaintance with attempts made to rebel against the power of England. They saw what was the end to the attempt made by O'Brien. They saw what was the end to the Whiteboy business ... It was fast in their minds that the end of the Fenian business would be the same – young men sailing on an unhappy course for a time and, then treachery, false testimony, blood money, hanging and transportation for these young Irish men ... The clergy and the priests understood this only too well and it was no wonder that they were trying to counsel the boys, to put them on the right course and keep them out of the Fenian bands.[44]

The heartbreak that the charge of not being patriots caused the priests is very clear. Peter O'Leary is a nationalist, a true patriot, and he has to justify the

Roman Catholic church's hostility to the Fenians with patriotic reasons. It was not easy, but this search was a real passion which consumed him. Some of the evidence he cites for his patriotism, like destroying a hostile newspaper, is moving because of its sheer puerility. He had read an article telling the world that he 'was a friend of … England and an enemy of Ireland' so he 'took hold of the paper, put it down on the ground and danced on it until it was in ribbons'.[45] Far more than hatred of the enemy, this gesture expresses his despair at not being accepted as a 'good patriot'.

The analysis could go further. The reasons put forward by O'Leary to a certain extent express the justifiable reaction of an experienced and well-trained activist faced with the mistakes of the leaders of nineteenth-century secret societies. Priests had far closer links with the peasant masses than with the urban intellectuals. They knew from experience that elitist secret societies were much more open to repression than well-rooted mass movements. The criticism of Fenianism is political rather than moral and reads like a plan of action. Canon O'Leary was certainly not a dreamer of the Michael O'Dempsey type. His claim that the clergy, with its accumulated experience and wisdom, was the most suitable body to provide the Irish people with leadership, even in political struggles, was a reasonable one. Such an interpretation is definitely confirmed by O'Leary's account of the agrarian struggles of which he was an unconditional supporter:

> There was nothing to prevent me giving advice to a congregation of farmers and telling them to go ahead with their movement. I realised that they were in need of counsel. They were all about me – sullen and dejected. The ancient terror still … Then a strong young priest from County Limerick came and went up on the platform. I myself went up with him. He began to speak and he was right good at it. He spoke boldly, explaining how the masters were doing an injustice to the farmers when they demanded rents that could not be made out of the land. The farmers listening to the speech were amazed that

someone had the nerve to tell the truth so outspokenly. As he was speaking, I was looking at them. More priests came. Every one, as he came, leaped up until there were so many of them there was hardly room for any more ... when the people saw the crush of priests up on the platform and each priest, as his turn came, speaking more boldly and dauntlessly than the person before him, the dejection, fear and mistrust began to go out of their faces.[46]

This episode proves O'Leary's contention that the clergy were the ideal leaders of the Irish people; without the priests, the peasant crowd was unprotected, leaderless, downtrodden, frightened and suffering from the age-old fear of the master:

The mass of small tenants ... understood very little of the land problem beyond the question of rent and the dread reality of eviction ... The people ... were the enemies of the system by force of Celtic instinct more than any process of independent thought or conviction.[47]

In the course of a meeting, an orator asks for the whole system of landlordism to be abolished. To whom should the rent then be paid asked a farmer.[49] Such naïvety has an inevitable consequence: the 'leader' must come from the outside, the priest able to express forcefully the grievances of the peasant world and being 'quite good at it'. 'The record of the clergy in their devotion to the people in times of trial, their superior education and intelligence, gave them this position as a matter of obvious fitness.'[49] They bring the liberating word – that word which awakens, enlightens and guides. They give heart to the people. The picture O'Leary paints of this peasant meeting is surprising, as there was not a single farmer on the platform on which the priests are crowded in serried ranks. Finally, perhaps, the sentiment which dominated this whole chapter is that of revenge. The day has gone when Peter O'Leary was limited to trampling a newspaper underfoot to prove his patriotism:

There was another great gladness on me, with an even

greater cause for it! At long last, the whole world was able
to see that the reason the priests had been against the
Fenians was not from any affection for the English nor for
fear of their law; and that a terrible injustice was done to
them when the opposite was said.[50]

At last the time had come, at last there was the vast
relief of being part of an anti-English movement, and,
furthermore, with the clergy occupying a leading position
in that movement.

For what purpose had the clergy assumed a leading
position? The search for influence in Irish peasant society
was not motivated by a desire to proselytise. The
influence of the church was an accomplished fact with
which no one dreamed of arguing. On the contrary, this
privileged social position allowed for an easier moulding
of the community, allowing the church to leave its
cultural work according to an overall plan in which
Roman Catholicism did not appear as the dominant
characteristic.

Peter O'Leary's efforts, in the successive parishes and
schools where he worked, were founded on the desire to
safeguard a 'simple' and 'natural' peasant society from
the temptations and vices of modernism. When writing of
the decline of Gaelic, he employs the emotionally-charged
term 'blight' to describe the crisis afflicting the
language.[51] The end of Irish is thus considered as a
cultural Famine, and like the Famine it is explained not
as the will of God but as the perverse foreign influence of
the English and 'modern society'. The renewal of the
Irish language would thus be an added guarantee of
protection against 'foreign' influence. To liberate his
country from these malignant influences the best weapon
is personal example. Here O'Leary falls in line with the
means of action recommended by Sinn Fein:

Whatever any other person might do, I would not let my
own amount of the language go to nothing. On the spot, I
began to say 'Mary's Crown' in Gaelic, like we used to do
at home and north in Derrynamona while I was there.
This kept me from getting out of practice with the

language. I began, also, to read it for myself from the books I'd get in the college library, and I used to write down anything that appealed to me in a little pocket-book.[52]

It should be noted that O'Leary's intimate inner knowledge of the workings of the village community prevented him from advocating an unworkable or utopian position. At no time does he suggest, for example, that Gaelic should become the only language spoken in Ireland. Political realism leads him to recommend bilingualism:

The people who had nothing but Gaelic had their minds pinioned where everyday business was concerned. For example, in any kind of legal affair the man with English was able to turn black and white on them and they had no means of defending themselves ... the man without English was in disastrous straits.[53]

It is on such particular points that the social and political break between the urban intellectuals and the priests is sharpest. The latter knew from experience that the best defenders of the peasants' interests were frequently those peasants who had learned English and were therefore able to stand up to English landlords; fighting an eviction in court or writing a threatening letter to an unjust landlord were, after all, actions to be undertaken in English. Arthur Griffith, meanwhile, was asking the Irish to pay more for products manufactured in Ireland if this was necessary to protect Irish industry, thereby ruling out the participation of the poor in the national struggle.

Peter O'Leary understood very well why the peasant used English as a means of combating the English landlord. Such realism and understanding created invaluable reciprocal links of confidence that no appeal to a sense of civic duty could replace. The same was true of other contexts in which the language was used. On one occasion when O'Leary was speaking at a Land League meeting he noticed a spy taking notes of his speech, and immediately switched to Irish. The crowd roared with laughter.[54] In this context, Irish no longer had anything to do with individual, interior, moral purity. It became a weapon. Amongst people who share such a weapon, an active confidence in one another comes into being. When Peter O'Leary received a letter from his bishop, who feared that his political activity might keep children away from school, his reply was a model of the relationship that could exist between culture and politics:

> Instead of it doing any damage to the school, my being in the Land League will benefit it. All the boys, who are coming to the school, are from farming families with the exception of two and the fathers of this pair have a great affection for the Land League.[55]

The Christian Brothers

O'Leary, of course, was both part and representative of the church as a whole. The Catholic church considered nationalism, especially its romantic brand, as a fierce competitor, as nationalism clearly shared some of the characteristics of religion. The church objected strongly to revolutionary ideas and to the use of violent methods in the fight for political independence, and it therefore had to show its nationalist credentials and re-establish its 'character' against the slander of those nationalists opposed to the 'power of the priest in politics'. Such ambiguities created tensions within the church itself. As the history of the Christian Brothers shows, conformity and defiance were both a necessity for political survival. Rome pressurised the Irish church and its old and conservative bishops to moderate the nationalist zeal of Irish priests. This tension could be resolved in exactly the same way as the tensions within the Irish society as a whole, in romantic nationalism. The textbooks used by the Christian Brothers were full of poems and songs glorifying nationalist violence in the past, and the Christian Brothers' schools could be shown to be a nationalist breeding ground:

The leaders who emerged in 1916 and the subsequent years were largely pupils of the Christian Brothers' schools ... Due recognition has not yet been given to the Irish Christian Brothers for their part in the nationalist struggle, particularly for their unqualified support of the Gaelic Revival.[56]

The National schools were founded in 1831 by the Whig ministry of Earl Grey with the aim of ending all state funding of proselytising societies and establishing a non-religious national system of education 'from which should be banished even the suspicion of proselytism'.[57] A new seven-strong Board of Education was established, and included among its members two Catholics. Priests of all denominations were allowed in the schools two days a week. The Catholic bishops were totally opposed to the scheme: they wanted what they still want today, Catholic schools for Catholic children, and therefore used the Christian Brothers' schools as an alternative to the National schools, thus becoming rebels once more against the godless English. The Christian Brothers' books were 'more Catholic and more nationalist than any other textbooks in Ireland', so not surprisingly the Christian Brothers' schools came to be regarded as the 'real national system' by the Catholic Irish.[58] The distinction was even greater as National schools, 'in order to avoid offending any religious grouping, deliberately omitted any mention of Catholicism or of Irish culture, geography, history and mythology'. In National school textbooks children read: 'On the east of Ireland is England where the Queen lives; many people who live in Ireland were born in England and we speak the same language and are called one nation.'[59] The Christian Brothers, on the other hand, taught their pupils about Irish resistance to English invasion, Irish suffering and English persecution, and the splendour of Gaelic civilisation. 'It was their teaching of history that was the crucial reason for their image as staunch patriots and for their great popularity among Irish nationalists.'[60]

The British government wanted, with the National school system, to impose a non-denominational education, but not a truly secular system since religious teaching would take place on the two days a week when priests were allowed into schools. The plan, obviously based on an enlightened British view of education, was tolerant, open-minded and opposed to the presence of religious images in schools. It was, in other words, the equivalent of Protestantism. Inspectors visiting these schools were constantly on the look-out for crucifixes and pious images. No wonder Cardinal Cullen declared he would deny the sacrements to parents who allowed their children to be educated in the lion's den.[61] Steeped in rebellion, the Christian Brothers' schools were considered by the Irish not only as Catholic schools but as nationalist schools as well. There was, in addition, a class dimension to the question: the other Catholic schools in Ireland, run by Jesuits and Dominicans, were middle-class establishments and considered as schools for West Britons, whereas the Christian Brothers catered for the urban poor:

> The leadership of the IRA came largely from those who got their education from the Christian Brothers, and got it free or at very little cost. This was the first generation of men of no property among whom secondary education was sufficiently diffused to provide the effective leadership for a revolution.[62]

What emerges very clearly from a study either of individuals like Peter O'Leary, or of orders like the Christian Brothers, is that the Catholic church competed with secular nationalism, but certainly not through a criticism of nationalism as an ideology or as a political attitude. Instead, Catholicism tried to imprint its own brand of nationalism as the only 'true' one. On the eve of the Second World War, for example, one finds discussions in the British Protestant churches which, under the influence of Christian pacifist ideas, were criticising nationalism as an attitude conducive to war. At the same time, the Irish Catholic church saw democracy and secularism as the cause of wars and held that the peoples of Europe had forgotten the Christian virtues.[63] 'We should be thankful that our country stands loyally for her Christian heritage; Eire proclaims her constitution "in the name of the Most Holy Trinity".'[64] Christian nationalism breeds peace – neutrality in the case of Ireland; secular nationalism breeds war.

Father Shaw and 1916

This struggle over the definition of nationalism has never ceased, and of course continues to the present day. A significant landmark in this fierce battle was the episode of the article written on the fiftieth anniversary of the Easter Rising by Father Shaw, then Professor of Irish Studies at University College, Dublin.[65] This article was commissioned for a special issue of *Studies* commemorating the Easter Rising but was then rejected as unsuitable for a commemorative issue. The article was finally published in 1972, two years after its author's death.

Father Shaw's presentation of the history of Ireland, and especially of the nationalist movement, is, quite frankly, naïve, crude, prejudiced and almost entirely lacking historical foundation; it cannot be described as a 'serious article' by an academic historian. It is, therefore, important to understand why this article aroused such controversy. It can hardly be claimed that 40-odd pages about the heroes and villains in Irish history deserved front-page news coverage followed by a review and editorial in the *Irish Times* on the grounds that it was a piece of serious historical scholarship. Yet the newspapers which gave extensive coverage to Father Shaw's ideas were not wrong in treating his article seriously: despite itself, it was a landmark in the history of ideas.

On a cursory reading, Father Shaw's ideas were not really particularly novel, and indeed they form part of a long-established tradition within the Catholic church. Like Peter O'Leary, Father Shaw faced the problem of trying to condemn the most spectacular aspects of Irish struggle against foreign oppression without being branded as an enemy of the national cause. The Fenians said repeatedly that they took their religion from Rome and their politics from Dublin; 'No priest in politics' was a well-known catch-phrase. Father Shaw, like Peter O'Leary, tried to reinstate the priest into Irish politics. This was a form of historical revisionism, but, unlike Conor Cruise O'Brien's *States of Ireland*, a classic example of secular revisionism, Shaw's was Catholic revisionism. Taking advantage of the changes taking place in Ireland in the 1960s and the growing rejection of some of the ideas on which the state was founded, Shaw sought to justify with hindsight the church's opposition to Fenianism and armed rebellion in general. He also went a decisive step further and criticised some of the fundamental tenets of nationalism.

This he did not through theoretical or historical analysis but in a moralising tone reminiscent of Peter O'Leary's patronising attitude towards the Irish peasantry. For Father Shaw, the physical force tradition was both morally and culturally wrong. Morally, because it was the breeding ground for violence and hatred, and nothing is more alien to Irish politics than keeping the fires of hatred burning, and culturally because he saw this tradition as alien to the Irish race.

According to Father Shaw, the anniversary, as promoted and celebrated by the media and by the state, was a history written in terms of heroes and villains in which the Fenians, that is to say a minority within the Irish people, a self-appointed elite who decided what was good and what was bad for the people, were the undisputed heroes. This view of history compels the Irish to consider unpatriotic the majority of their ancestors, those who did not share the new-fangled revolutionary ideas and instead agreed to be led by their church, those who preferred peaceful means to armed violence. All this is a tremendous hoax. The typical Irishman was not revolutionary. Revolution was an Anglo-Irish affair, and the Anglo-Irish used the Irish as pawns in their nefarious game. It was particularly clear to Father Shaw that the 1916 Rising was a minority movement, a rising of the city against the country, of the Anglo-Irish against the Gaels.

Father Shaw pursued his argument with a study of the prophets of this alien tradition. Wolfe Tone had fought for separation from Britain and the introduction of French Republican ideas into Ireland. Tone's gospel was one of hatred. His dislike of England, composed exclusively of hatred and having no love in it, was not truly Irish. Christ, Shaw wrote, came to free slaves from no other chains than those of their sins, not from national oppression.[66] Tone's hatred of England was not truly Irish, since it was rooted in personal grievances against Pitt. That Tone was not of truly Irish stock was proved by the fact that he had abandoned his wife and children. He did not know or understand Gaelic Ireland, despised its culture, its religion and its church. The Catholic church represented for him an obstacle to revolutionary ideas. In a nutshell, Tone's supreme sacrifice must not be allowed to conceal the fact that his views were alien to Irish soil and to Irish blood.

The whole of Father Shaw's argument was based on the simplistic equation anti-Catholic = anti-Irish. He was particularly severe about the slander against Catholic bishops who were branded lackeys of the English because they condemned the Fenians. For Shaw, these men had been possessed of sufficient courage to condemn the 'unhealthy' ideas of Tone and remained faithful to Christian ideas in their endeavour to protect the Irish people from bloodshed.[67] For Father Shaw as for Peter O'Leary, the true friends of the people are those who avoid murderous head-on clashes with the English.

Shaw believed that Patrick Pearse brought two new ideas to Irish nationalism: firstly, that Ireland free must be Ireland Gaelic, and secondly, the transformation of nationalism into a sacred quest. On those two counts, Father Shaw demonstrated that Pearse was no more a true Irishman than Wolfe Tone. He was not well versed in Irish cultural and literary traditions. The heroes of the past that Pearse held up to Irish youth (Cuchulain and Colmcille) were drawn directly from Standish O'Grady, the creator of a fantasy version of Irish history, without any critical sifting. Pearse found his heroes in mythology not in history. This idea is reminiscent of the criticism of the promoters of the Celtic revival as a band of plunderers who tried to revive an alien literature with Irish ghosts.

Shaw's fundamentally and radically new idea was that nationalism as such is alien to the Irish tradition. The idea of an Irish nation was alien to the people. They were preoccupied with freedom on a personal and local level, but not with national freedom. Cuchulain, Shaw emphasised, died fighting other Irishmen, not foreign invaders. More recently, the sacrifices of men for their country have acquired prominence, but Shaw reminds his readers that more Irishmen had been killed fighting alongside the English than fighting against them. The truth is that Pearse's notions were based on a sham: the idea of an eternal national feeling in people's souls. The Irish fought for their religious beliefs, for their homes and for their land, for their lives or the food they and their families needed, but they did not belong to a world in which national sovereignty was vested in armed force. It is very clear for Shaw that the Catholic church was not opposed to a particular brand of nationalism but to the very idea of nationalism because it meant a secular isation of politics as it did in all European countries where it prevailed. It became possible, as Patrick Pearse made clear, to believe in one's country as one believed in God, and to sacrifice one's life for one's country to save and redeem it, exactly as Jesus had sacrificed his life. Nationalism therefore has to be made alien in order to leave the field clear for Catholic ways of thinking.

Such an argument can only be pursued at the price of a serious distortion of Irish history. The most important consequences of English control of Ireland are muffled, the part played by the Catholic church and its inner contradictions in relation to the national struggle are ignored, and the revolutionary elements in nationalism are denied.

The history of Ireland that emerges is a most surprising one. The Famine is hardly mentioned. The Home Rule crisis is presented as a purely domestic affair, and there seems to be no relation between the Ulster Volunteers and the rest of the United Kingdom. In the case of Wolfe Tone, since he was 'anti-Catholic', no mention is made of his stance against discriminatory laws. The fact that Ireland was considered as the stepping-stone for the reconquest of the British Isles by Roman Catholicism, and that many Irish people therefore adopted a cautious attitude towards separatism, is waved aside. The internal, 'Irish', contradictions of society are not worth mentioning, and the lock-out and the strike of 1913 disappear from view. The fight waged by Michael Davitt and the Land League is mentioned, but not the violent outrages and boycotts, all condemned by the Catholic church in their time. The Land League's nationalism is also erased: if Irish peasants sometimes shot their landlords, this was not because they were English, but simply because they were bad landlords.

By removing the social content from nationalism, by ignoring the fact that it was a social movement, Father Shaw reduced it to a religion, and so a competitor with another religion, Catholicism. One or the other must disappear. But the separation of Catholicism and nationalism was far too dangerous for the Catholic church in Ireland and Father Shaw's heretical ideas were allowed to die with him.

Half a century later, James McDyer, a priest and creator of the co-operative of Glencolumbkille, trod the same path as Peter O'Leary and the Christian Brothers, rather than that marked out by Father Shaw. Born into a poor Donegal family, educated in a Catholic school, the only way to achieve his dreams was through the priesthood. He assumes without any hesitation that for a poor young man becoming a priest is a major rise in social status: 'Priests were always treated with very great respect and veneration and there could have been in my motivation a certain amount of looking up to, a hero-worship of the priest, he was so respected in our house.'[68] In trying to help the local community to set up co-operative enterprises, he finds himself in the same role of leader as Canon O'Leary. The peasants are passive and demoralised. The most ambitious and most energetic have emigrated. So McDyer had to assume the role of 'overlord' and of 'benevolent dictator'.[69] He even goes as far as to accept being described as a Messiah: 'If you mean by the word someone who spearheads ideas and actions, yes, I am a sort of Messiah.'[70] If McDyer is no longer in the mainstream of Catholicism, it is not because of his ideological stance. It is simply because rural Ireland has gone and contemporary Irish society accepts him as a nostalgic figure rather than as a man of the future.

Notes

1   De Valera speaking in the Dail, 6 July 1939 in Maurice Moynihan (ed.), *Speeches and Statements by de Valera, 1917–1973*, Dublin 1980.

2   Conor Cruise O'Brien (ed.), *The Shaping of Modern Ireland*, London 1970, p. 21.

3   Sean O'Casey, *Irish Worker*, 22 February 1913, reproduced in Robert Hogan (ed.), *Feathers from the Green Crow, 1905–1925*, London 1963.

4   W.B. Yeats, *Autobiographies, Reveries over Childhood and Youth*, London 1970, p. 18.

5   Ibid., p. 31.

6   Ibid., p. 61.

7   W.B. Yeats, *Mythologies*, London 1970, p. 139.

8   W.B. Yeats, *Autobiographies*, p. 31.

9   Revd Peter McKevitt, 'The Beveridge Plan Reviewed', *Irish Ecclesiastical Record*, March 1943.

10   W.B. Yeats, *Mythologies*.

11   Ibid., pp. 72–3.

12   W.B. Yeats, *Autobiographies*, p. 155.

13   Tomas O Crohan, *The Islandman*, London 1934, p. 322.

14   Peig Sayers, *An Old Woman's Reflections*, London 1962, p. 12.

15   W.B. Yeats, *Autobiographies*, p. 201.

16   Michel Leiris, 'L'ethnographie devant le colonialisme' in *Cinq*

Etudes d' Ethnologie, Paris 1969.

17 AE (G.W. Russell), *The Building of a Rural Civilisation*, Dublin 1910, p. xx.

18 Michael Collins, *The Path to Freedom*, Cork 1968, pp. 98–9 and 127.

19 O Crohan, op. cit., p. 196.

20 Maurice O'Sullivan, *Twenty Years A-Growing*, Oxford 1970, p. x.

21 O Crohan, op. cit., pp. 7 and 13.

22 O'Sullivan, op. cit., pp. 142 and 154.

23 Ibid., Chapter VI.

24 O Crohan, op. cit., my emphasis.

25 See George Thomson's preface to O'Sullivan's *Twenty Years A-Growing*.

26 Hugh Brody, *Inishkillane, Change and Decline in the West of Ireland*, Harmondsworth 1973, p. 1.

27 Ibid., p. 13.

28 Robert Creswel, *Une Commune Rurale d'Irlande*, Paris 1969, p. 122.

29 AE (G.W. Russell), *The National Being, Some Thoughts on an Irish Policy*, Dublin and London 1916, pp. 125 and 176.

30 D.P. Moran, *The Philosophy of Irish Ireland*, Dublin 1905, p. 10.

31 Michael Davitt, *The Fall of Feudalism in Ireland or the Story of the Land League Revolution*, New York 1904, p. 100.

32 Ibid., p. 175.

33 Ibid., p. 652.

34 Archbishop Croke, *Freeman's Journal*, 31 May 1880, cited in ibid., p. 262.

35 O Crohan, op. cit., pp. 115–6.

36 Frank O'Connor, *An Only Child*, London 1970, p. 129.

37 Peter O'Leary, *My Story*, Cork 1970 (first published 1915).

38 Brinsley MacNamara, *The Valley of the Squinting Windows*, Tralee 1968 (first published 1918).

39 C.T. O Ceirin, introduction to O'Leary, *My Story*, p. 14.

40 Ibid.

41 Ibid., p. 21.

42 Ibid., p. 29.

43 Ibid., pp. 71–2.

44 Ibid., p. 86.

45 Ibid., p. 83.

46 Ibid., pp. 113–5.

47 Davitt, op. cit., pp. 160–2.

48 Ibid., p. 164.

49 Ibid., p. 466.

50 O'Leary, op. cit., p. 115.

51 Ibid., p. 73.

52 Ibid.

53 Ibid., p. 148.

54 Ibid., p. 124.

55 Ibid., p. 119.

56 Barry Coldrey, *Faith and Fatherland, The Christian Brothers and the Development of Irish Nationalism, 1838–1921*, Dublin 1988,

pp. 2 and 3.

57　Ibid., p. 26.

58　Ibid., p. 28.

59　Ibid., p. 59.

60　Ibid., p. 113.

61　Ibid., pp. 35–6.

62　C.S. Andrews, cited in ibid., p. 89.

63　Maurice Goldring, 'Les Eglises de Belfast Pendant la Seconde Guerre Mondiale', *Etudes Irlandaises*, June 1991.

64　Bishop Magee, pastoral letter, Belfast, 15 February 1942.

65　Father Shaw, 'The Canon of Irish History – A Challenge', *Studies*, Summer 1972.

66　Ibid., p. 123.

67　Ibid., p. 129.

68　Father McDyer, *Irish Times*, 10 January 1976.

69　Father McDyer of Glencolumbkille, *An Autobiography*, Dingle 1982.

70　Father McDyer, *Irish Times*, 10 January 1976.

4 Intellectuals and Labour

When Davitt, Griffith, Collins, O'Leary, Yeats and George Russell wrote and talked about the Irish peasantry, they were really talking among themselves and about themselves, debating who would rule the new nation which was being born. The peasants sang, danced and told stories, they demonstrated and boycotted; very conveniently for the Dublin intellectuals, they did not intervene in the cultural debates of the day. Not so with the workers of Dublin. They had a voice: trade unions which they themselves led, political parties under the leadership of their own kin, people like James Larkin, who made fine speeches, like the village priests, and even, like James Connolly, wrote articles and books. Could the conclusion be drawn, then, that what the intellectuals construed as authentic in Irish peasants was in fact their silence and that, in so far as workers gave themselves a voice, they were no longer 'authentic' but influenced by corrupting foreign influences?

According to Tom Garvin, in early twentieth-century Ireland the groups competing for power were the Anglo-Irish, who hoped 'to retain some shreds of their social and political influence', the Ulster Unionists, who 'opted not to compete but to construct another arena', the new Catholic middle class and the Catholic clergy. Labour was out, while big business was mostly Unionist in politics and, concentrated in the North, had in effect side-stepped conflict.[1]

Cultural nationalism was about the creation of the fundamental values of the nation and all the groups

competing for power presented themselves as the true
defenders of the national interest. Labour had not always
been absent from the struggle for power, as was seen in
the 1913 strike and lock-out in Dublin. Intellectuals kept
a long-lasting silence on issues affecting the urban
working class. Urban workers were considered as having
no values or folklore, no *Volkgeist* or *Volkkunst*, although
perhaps it was because they had all of these, and they
could express them without any outside help, because
they had a voice, it was judged better not to stir up what
might well prove to be a hornets' nest.

Class ethnocentrism is always extreme in groups
competing for power: privileges, whether those already in
existence or those being created, have to be justified,
morally and culturally. Populism as seen in attitudes to
the world of the peasantry was another way of expressing
this class ethnocentrism: it was simply the inversion of
dominant values which all kinds of populism have in
common. The people have an authentic culture; they, 'the
people' are worth more than us, the upper crust of
society.[2] Intellectuals were thus designating as 'the
people' a voiceless peasantry whose true values the
intellectuals themselves were the best placed to express
since they recognised their authenticity.

Working-class culture was less authentic above all
because it existed and had a voice, albeit a muffled one:
William Thompson, the first Irish socialist and feminist,
Fergus O'Connor and J. Bronterre O'Brien, Irish leaders
of the Chartist movement in Britain, Fintan Lalor and
Michael Davitt, were all influenced by, or influential in
the development of socialist ideas. George Russell was
inspired by the co-operative movement and the Fenian
James Stephens had been connected with the First
International. These men were not, however, potential
leaders of the nation or major influences on international
labour. The only occasion when there was a real
encounter between intellectuals and organised labour in
Ireland was during the Dublin strike and lock-out of
1913, a period which repays further study.

Dublin 1913

'The most tragic and most bitter confrontation between the forces of capital and labour that this country has ever seen,' is one historian's melancholy verdict on the events of 1913.[3] The issues involved were clear-cut: the workers wanted to join Jim Larkin's union, and William Murphy, the nationalist leader of the Dublin employers, sacked those who did so. The conflict became a major one, so much so that it worked as a dividing line between all social, political and ideological forces. Every Dubliner had to choose where he or she stood; the whirlwind carried away all attempts at neutrality. The strikers were ready to die for the cause, Murphy and his employers' federation were, in the most literal sense, quite prepared to starve them out. The church, the British labour movement, political organisations, writers and the cultural movement all had to choose; everybody had to 'come off the fence'.[4]

A notable feature of the conflict as people saw it at the time was the participation of intellectuals. For W.P. Ryan, 'the incoming of men more socially favoured to help [was] a new feature in labour struggles in the capital'.[5] James Connolly had earlier deplored that 'men of letters', instead of becoming the champions of Irish workers and observers of their social conditions, were occupied elsewhere, and 'the working class left without any means of influencing outside public opinion'.[6] That regret was now superseded and Connolly's paper welcomed the storm roused by literary giants:

> Men like Yeates [*sic*], George Russell ('AE'), Bernard Shaw have torn off the mask ... the recognised abilities of our song writers and of the creators of a new era in literature are given with the 'pent-up love of their hearts' to the cause for which Larkin fought.[7]

As if to comply with James Connolly's wish, Dublin intellectuals became sociologists and 'observers of workers' conditions'. The *Irish Review* regularly published articles about urban deprivation; Suzanne R. Day wrote about workhouse children while Maud Gonne described the plight of children who attended school from 9 a.m. to 3 p.m. without having had breakfast. There were also numerous examples of practical involvement in the conflict. During autumn 1913, leading characters in the literary world took part in a variety of charitable or solidarity actions. Constance Markievicz spent her days in Liberty Hall giving out meals; her home, Surrey House, was used as shelter and hiding place by both Larkin and Connolly, and Connolly recovered in the house after his hunger strike and release from prison.[8] Maude Gonne organised her Ladies' School Committee for starving children. The Dublin Gaelic Athletic Association collected thirteen guineas for the 'starving children of Dublin' at its 1913 conference. Adelaide Needham, a famous singer, performed at a concert to raise funds for those suffering because of the strike.[9]

Soup kitchens, solidarity, concerts and ladies' committees might be dismissed as trivial, but the people of Dublin were poor and desperate for food, and it should be remembered that hunger was the main weapon of Murphy and the Dublin employers in their battle to wear down the strikers' resistance. The uncomplicated humanitarian character of this support for the strikers and their families should not therefore be dismissed but, rather, be seen as an index of middle-class public opinion. The scope of the solidarity is a good measure of the relative isolation of the employers. One should also remember, in considering the charitable help given by the urban middle classes, that charity as always, was a contentious area. Archbishop Walsh claimed that indiscriminate charity could become a source of demoralisation: 'Hundreds of poor parents ... if left to take care of their children themselves, would be able and willing to make the effort.'[10]

Another way in which Dublin intellectuals were able to intervene was as go-betweens between the two parties in the various conciliation and peace committees. In October 1913, 'Certain citizens of Dublin who declined to accept ... abdication of reason and enthronement of blind violence, met together and formed the Peace Committee.'[11] Among its members were to be found T.M.Kettle, Culverwell, F.W. Ryan, Oliver Saint John Gogarty, Thomas MacDonagh, Padric Colum, Joseph Plunkett and W.B. Yeats, self-deprecatingly described by Kettle himself as 'a set of academic busybodies'. A letter to the press gives an indication of the social composition of the committee: 'I am neither a poet, a painter, a philosopher, nor a professor ... But I would ... fain ... set the part of a peacemaker.'[12] All those men were terrified by the violence of conflict, by the 'ruin' of their city, the seemingly never-ending deadlock, and they wished to launch an appeal to public opinion in order to secure a truce between the two parties and the resumption of talks. The first public meeting took place on 7 October 1913. In his opening speech, Professor Kettle insisted on the non-partisan character of the undertaking. Dublin was being ruined by extremism on both sides. They were there to put the views of a middle party: the citizens of Dublin. When one orator, Miss Harrison, expressed her wish that the employers had not rejected the conclusions of the Askwith Commission, the chairman interrupted her so as to maintain the spirit of neutrality.[13]

A three-strong deputation from the Peace Committee (Professors Kettle and Culverwell and Joseph Plunkett), met the employers on 13 October 1913. As a token of its good will, the Dublin Trades Council had signed the following document:

> That this executive, representing the workers in the present dispute, authorises the Peace Committee to seek for an intermediary to bring out a conference of the parties to this conflict, and stands ready to attend such a conference should their efforts meet with success.[14]

Their efforts failed. Another public meeting, held for the same purpose, was chaired by the Lord Mayor and received a message of support from Archbishop Walsh.

The only partisan statement came from an aristocrat, The O'Mahony, who claimed that one man – Jim Larkin – could not single-handedly cause such a prolonged dispute. If the workers were showing such determination, this was because their demands were well-grounded.

The Peace Committee's deputation was a failure. On 11 November 1913, the committee published a statement: it had tried to draw the two parties nearer but had failed. When the committee decided to suspend its activities the blame for the failure was placed on the employers' federation. The *Irish Times* denounced the partisan character of the statement. Professor Culverwell, one of the leaders of the Peace Committee, felt intimidated and retreated, apportioning the blame equally between the two parties, adding, 'Our educational system is lamentably at fault, since it gives no guidance to employers and employed.'[15] The professor was back on the fence.

The Dublin Trades Council varied in its assessment of the Peace Committee. On 1 October, it agreed to be represented by the committee, but on 25 October the *Irish Worker* printed the word 'peace' between inverted commas and attacked Tom Kettle and Joseph Plunkett in very harsh terms: Tom Kettle's father, Andrew Kettle, was presented as an organiser of strike-breakers and Joseph Plunkett's mother, who protested against the transportation of children to Britain, was denounced as a slum-owner. The unsigned article asked Kettle and Plunkett to apply their 'reforming zeal' on their own families. James Connolly, however, considered the intervention of the Peace Committee in a positive light: 'The way out of this deadlock is for all sides to consent to the formation of a conciliation board, before which all disputes must be brought,' he wrote, thus adopting the committee's proposal.[16] When all hope of conciliation was abandoned, in December, he recalled that the employer's stand was

denounced by every enlightened public opinion in these islands, by the whole trade union world; by the public of Dublin; by the press of Great Britain; by the report of Sir

George Askwith; by the verdict of the Industrial Peace Committe.[17]

The committee's epitaph was written by Padric Colum: 'The Dublin Industrial Peace Committee has dissolved itself. When one party in dispute is bent upon securing not a settlement, but a surrender, there is no place for honest go-betweens.'[18]

The part played by intellectuals in 1913 is very revealing of the state of the country and of the political expectations of the educated urban middle class as a group. The strikers demanded the right to organise as they wished. This was scarcely a 'revolutionary' demand, and the acceptance by the trade unions of the Askwith Report showed the essential moderation of their position. As one leader of the Peace Committee observed, 'The workers have talked wildly and acted calmly; the employers have talked calmly and acted wildly.'[19] The strikers had accepted the Peace Committee as a go-between to prove their good-will, but nothing short of total victory seemed to satisfy the employers in general and Murphy in particular. In the autumn of 1913, Dublin seemed to be the stage of a pre-industrial dispute, of a war between the aristocracy and the peasantry, the outcome of which could only be wholesale slaughter. Unlike their British colleagues, Irish entrepreneurs had not yet learned that the recognition of organised labour and negotiation with trade unions is less costly than the savage denial of trade union rights which leaves the workers no choice between sporadic uprisings and total submission. In the 1913 conflict it appears that the labour movement in Dublin was able to learn from the experience of its British counterpart, but the employers were in no state to learn from the experience of their British equivalents. This was certainly not a sign of strength on the employers' part.

The relative weakness of industrial capital in early twentieth-century Ireland was not unique. In Britain industrial entrepreneurs had grown up in a relatively

hostile environment; until the end of the nineteenth
century, parliament and state were dominated by the
landed aristocracy, and industrial and financial interests
were represented by land. In Southern Ireland, where
the industrial revolution had developed slowly and,
indeed, been hindered by the union with Britain,
entrepreneurs were still lacking political power and
self-assurance. William Murphy never ceased to fight for
recognition of the importance of his class, in an endless
crticism of dominant values in the country, according to
which, 'It was less than respectable to devote one's life to
the making of money. Industry was crippled by the social
class who made a fortune and then gave up the business
out of a sense of snobbishness.'[20] Tom Kettle tried to
understand the position in which Dublin businessmen
found themselves:

> The ordinary Dublin employer is neither so big nor so bad
> ... The pageant of luxury ... is provided mainly by the
> professional and annuitant classes. Your ordinary Dublin
> employer is not a man of very luxurious or Capuan habits
> of life. He is not a Napoleon, nor even a captain of
> industry ... He experiences ... the acute reality of foreign
> competition ... his customers denounce him, his workers
> denounce him, finding himself vulnerable at every point,
> he enlists under the leadership of the unvulnerable
> Chairman of the Tramway Company [i.e. Murphy].[21]

In his famous 'Address to the Masters of Dublin', George
Russell was rather more critical of the city's businessmen, but stressed the same points: 'You are
incompetent in the sphere of industry ... your enterprises
have been dwindling ... You are bad citizens, not wealthy
enough to endow our city with munificent gifts.'[22]

Hypertrophy on the part of intellectuals in this
dispute is an indication of that relative weakness. It is
striking that all attempts at conciliation were consisten-
tly negative in their view of the employers and positive in
their attitude to the strikers. The *Irish Times* and the
Freeman's Journal wrote patronisingly of the businessmen as hard-working and deserving but lacking

experience, incapable of dealing with dangerous troublemakers.

The efforts of the Industrial Peace Committee may therefore be seen as an attempt to occupy a vacant space. The urban middle classes ('the enlightened section of the Dublin citizens'), were more than would-be intermediaries: they saw themselves as the potential leaders of Irish society. In classical political theory, the state is seen as an honest broker between classes, a national council of conciliation, and that is precisely how the Industrial Peace Committee presented itself. The employers were not sufficiently strong, experienced or educated to represent the general interest, but, rather, parochial and small-minded. The members of the Industrial Peace Committee, on the other hand, were educated and respectable, able to play the part of honest brokers. Thus, the dissolution of the Peace Committee was immediately followed by a Dublin Civil League founded by Justin Dempsey. In an earlier letter to the press, Dempsey had declared that capitalists were organised, workers had their unions, and asked, 'Who will be the Karl Marx of the middle class?'.[23] The answer, not surprisingly, was Justin Dempsey, leader of a 'thoroughly representative' new committee which 'commands the respect of every class of the community', and the first duty of organised middle class, according to its founder, was 'to prevent outbreaks of strikes and the use of lock-outs by capital ... Strong measures should, if necessary, be resorted to in order to bring the recalcitrant party to reason.'[24] Who could take strong measures, if not the state?

Encounters

Those Dublin intellectuals who tried to analyse the workers' conditions and struggles in depth were few and far between. Francis Sheehy-Skeffington was a member of this minority, and for him sympathy strikes were legitimate weapons of the working class which restored some balance of power with their opponents. James Stephens was an intellectual who had taken up Connolly's ideas in *Labour in Irish History* and claimed that, 'On the social development, the moral and material progress of the masses of the people, must surely depend the real worth and glory of a state.'[25] No wonder he supported the workers in the conflict: 'By bettering your own conditions, you are going to better the conditions of everyone.'[26]

In greater number were those who made the dispute part of their own national and cultural struggles. The nature of the conflict, its verbal and street violence, made this possible. The most extreme republicans considered the clashes with the police as simply the latest episodes in the heroic centuries-old struggle for the liberation of the country. The workers were heroes, the heirs of Oscar and Cuchulain.[27] When Jim Larkin was tried in the Green Street Court, Constance Markievicz recalled that the same tribunal was one of the last stages of Emmet's calvary.[28] George Russell saw the workers of Dublin as the vanguard of the co-operative movement that would sweep aside the captains of industry.[29] Maud Gonne explained that the roots of the dispute lay in Ireland's serfdom: 'In a free country, employers of labour would never have dared to propose [such a document] ... In Ireland they are protected by a police force over which Ireland had no control.'[30] Pearse hammered away with familiar ideas:

> [The workers] cannot punish the police brutes with empty hands against batons or stones against bullets. We often advised the people of Ireland to arm themselves, and we shall press upon them the wisdom of this course upon every [occasion].

In his speech at the Industrial Peace Committee's 13 October meeting, W.B. Yeats stated that he was one of the directors of a theatre which the strike was preventing from working normally and therefore wished to see a swift settlement of the dispute, a somewhat ambiguous expression of support.[31]

The seemingly unlikely alliance between trade unions and intellectuals in the Hugh Lane affair is not as odd as it might first appear to have been. Hugh Lane, an Anglo-Irish art-collector, wanted to donate his paintings to the City of Dublin, on condition that a gallery be built to house them. The offer met with strong opposition, led by William Murphy on the grounds that Lane was not 'a true Irishman'. The core of Lane's collection was composed of paintings by French Impressionists: Lane was not only 'a foreigner', he had 'un-Irish', cosmopolitan tastes.

Yeats wrote his protest in the guise of a poem published in the press:

> Romantic Ireland's dead and gone
> It's with O'Leary in the grave.[32]

On 31 July 1913, Jim Larkin moved a motion:

> That this Trades Council calls upon the Aldermen and Councillors of this City to accept the generous offer of Sir Hugh Lane. And further it is our opinion that the foul methods resorted to by the opposition to the erection of the Gallery is worthy of the chief instigator of the opposition; that it is not a question of a site ... The primary reason is to deny the working-class access to avenues of advancement and to limit the opportunities of unemployed men getting useful work.[32]

Was this alliance simply an historical freak? On the contrary, it seems that the entry of the labour movement on the stage of Dublin's political and social life was felt by intellectuals as a powerful lever with which to lift the lid of narrow-mindedness and bigotry. Before the dispute started, the *Irish Review* had saluted the publishing of the *Irish Worker* as another blow against Irish dogmatism.[34] A year earlier, in 1912, in a review of W.P. Ryan's *The Pope's Green Island*, Francis Sheehy-Skeffington had voiced the same idea:

Irish clericalism will meet its nemesis at the hands of the
Irish labour movement, which, by simply going about its
own business and ignoring the fury which the clergy must
continue to lavish upon it, will prove an effective
shattering force.[35]

W.B. Yeats, in his speech at the Industrial Peace
Committee's 13 October meeting, and in the *Irish Worker*
insisted on the necessity of the fight against those who
used religious fanaticism in order to break labour
organisations. How can one avoid imagining that he had
other quarrels and disputes in mind when he used the
phrase 'religious fantaticism'? AE fumed against the
industrialists as a class without culture, as was shown by
their artistic tastes.[36]

In the same way as the plays and the poems of the Irish
literati were condemned as 'un-Irish', British solidarity
in 1913 was viewed with suspicion and hostility. The food
cargoes sent by English unions were considered by the
Catholic church as a plot against Ireland's traditional
values. 'The cackle of the old souper has found a more oily
setting,' wrote the *Freeman's Journal*.[37] When Mrs
Montefiore organised the sending of Irish children to
English families, her project was solemnly and roundly
condemned by Archbishop Walsh:

> They can be no longer worthy of the name of Catholic
> mothers if they so far forget that duty as to send away
> their children to be cared for in a strange land, without
> security of any kind that those to whom the poor children
> are to be handed over are Catholics, or indeed, are
> persons of any faith at all.[38]

This statement unleashed a hysterical campaign against
the 'kidnapping' of Catholic children. The writers, who
had so often been the targets of similar campaigns,
rushed to take up their positions. At the Albert Hall
meeting calling for Larkin's release from prison, George
Russell and George Bernard Shaw spoke on the same
platform as Ben Tillett and James Connolly. Shaw, as
was his wont, made his case ironically: 'There were some

dwellings in Dublin that if they took the children out of them, the adults would misbehave themselves.' AE introduced himself as 'a Dublin man who came to apologise for the priests of Dublin ... [who said] it would be better to starve than leave the Christian atmosphere of Dublin'.[39]

The old quarrel had resumed: if speakers exposed the living conditions of the Dublin working class, 'Ireland was being defiled and blackened ... in the tradition of Irish cockneydom.'[40] It was easy for the writers to recognise the vilifications. They had been blamed for writing for the English, for exposing the foibles of the Irish people to please foreigners and for indulging in muck-raking. The arguments employed against their plays and novels were ready-made against syndicalism. In the *Catholic Bulletin*, articles devoted to the 'social question' dwelt at length on the subject of 'bad' versus 'good' literature. The vigilante committee which endeavoured to keep godless literature out of the country was cheered for its good work because the very future of the true faith was at stake 'if the spiritual life of the people is allowed to be slowly sapped away by the filthy and infidel literature that is now doing the work which souperism never could accomplish'.[41] And if this analogy between literature and syndicalism seems far-fetched, let it be clear that the confusion was very deliberate:

> For the past twenty years, the Gael has been crying ... for help to bear back the anglicisation he saw dragging its slimy length along – the immoral literature, the smutty post-cards, the lewd plays and the suggestive songs were bad, yet they were mere puffs from the fouled breath of paganised society. The full sewerage is now discharged upon us. The black devil of socialism, hoof and horn is amongst us.[42]

Although George Bernard Shaw set the hall laughing in London when he said, 'Being an intelligent Irishman, I left Ireland when I was twenty,' one can understand that the reaction was not quite the same in Dublin, and the *Freeman's Journal* presented the meeting as 'anti-Irish and anti-Christian'.[43] The same paper clearly bracketed writers and trade unionists together:

> The orations of the intellectuals and the syndicalists ... should open the eyes ... The Dublin workers ... are pawns in a larger game ... The feelings of the workers are being inflamed against almost every ideal and every principle of Ireland's social and political life.[44]

In this all too brief alliance between trade unionists and intellectuals gathered on the same platforms in Dublin and London, the cement was more than mere solidarity. It was the perception of a shared interest between the workers who wanted the freedom to organise as they wished, and men of letters who sought to defend their artistic freedom against the limitations of bigotry. As Desmond Ryan put it:

> It is easy enough to win applause in Ireland if the writer consents to deal with any subject more than ten years old, to curry favour with the political party for the moment on top, to remember all the sex, moral, political and religious taboos.[45]

This alliance found its most significant voice in 1913. By their active participation in the fight alongside Dublin's working people, the writers were struggling for their own freedom against the Holy Alliance for whom the only good worker is an obedient one and the only good writer is a servile one. Censorship and exile were weapons used against the social as well as against the literary vanguard. The demonstrators who howled on the Dublin quays against Mrs Montefiore and 'godless English families' had already trained their voices baying against godless plays in the theatres.

Labour Intellectuals

> Mr Parnell is the Moses of the lost children of Erin. He will, like Joshua, take them to the promised land of Home Rule, and then, with the Aaron's rod of peasant proprietary, he will strike the rock of landlordism.[46]

Peter O'Leary and other priests on the platforms at the Land League meeting could also be given the name Moses, while those who aspired to lead the lost children of the Dublin tenements bore the names of Larkin and Connolly. A study of their background is essential for an understanding of this group of 'working-class intellectuals'.

Labour leaders travelled, and travelled well. Like writers and other intellectuals, they found abroad a set of people with whom they could keep the home fire and familiar ideas burning. 'Foreign' trade unions, whether the syndicalist 'Wobblies' in the United States or the British trade unions, were their universities. When James Connolly, Michael Davitt or Jim Larkin were in Britain or America, they were not in exile in the sense Lenin was when in Zurich, but, rather, 'at home' in an enlarged homeland. Britain was certainly no more alien to these particular migrants than Dublin was for peasant incomers from the West of Ireland, but they became an integral part of Irish life and history in so far as they could prove their lives and deeds that they were good patriots, members of the 'Irish race'.

The terms of Connolly's famous controversy with the American socialist Daniel De Leon are very clear in this respect.[47] Although well known, the details of the controversy matter less than the fact that Connolly's arguments can be read as proof of his belief that the link with Ireland must be maintained at all costs. Bebel's famous *Women and Socialism*, first published in 1879, would not have met a warm welcome in Catholic Ireland, and its publication by a socialist journal in the United States was unacceptable to Connolly the Irishman. Connolly believed in monogamy and the sacred institution of marriage. Love and sex are private matters and socialism should not meddle with them. As far as Connolly was concerned, a socialist party's legitimate area of activity was the solid ground of class struggle, and if it abandoned this terrain it ran the risk of finding itself enmeshed in struggles led by the bourgeoisie. It is possible, of course, to explain Connolly's attitude as a direct consequence of a Catholic upbringing and traditional sexual relations. Connolly's social and cultural conservatism is well illustrated by the fact that he did not want his wife to work, and when she took in laundry or cleaned neighbours' houses in an effort to make ends meet, she had to conceal this work from her husband.[48]

Given the nature of Irish religious culture, anything that might link socialism and sexual permissiveness, socialism and free thought, would have rendered socialism unacceptable in the country. 'New-fangled ideas' such as De Leon's were therefore abhorrent to James Connolly. Socialism should not meddle with sex or religion. While working and agitating in America, Connolly was more concerned with his return home than with his political prospects in the United States. His paper, the *Workers' Republic*, was published for Ireland, not for America, 'and if the comrades in Minneapolis thought we were going to publish the paper to suit American politics, they were greatly mistaken'.[49] His alienation from American struggles did not worry him, as he wrote in a letter to William O'Brien:

> I have formed a fairly well developed plan of action for Ireland and I am afraid many non-Irish socialists would not understand it, and I am certain that their failure to do so would not cause my soul any uneasiness.[50]

The second eloquent example of these working-class leaders' desire to maintain strong links with the fundamental features of Irish culture is the way in which Connolly and Larkin approached the British labour movement during the 1913 lock-out when the difference in cultural attitudes towards Britain and the United States became an important political factor.

Initially, however, it is necessary to make a general observation. Emigration to America was considered to be noble, while emigration to Britain was not. At the time of the Famine, the choice of America as a destination seems to have been as much a cultural decision as an economic one: Britain was the oppressing country, while America was the land of liberty which had fought to free itself from England; Britain was a Protestant country, America a land of religious tolerance; Britain was harsh on its immigrant workers while America was a land of opportunity.[51] Those who went to Liverpool were considered as both materially and morally destitute. At the time of the Famine, the Poor Law did not apply to Ireland, so the system as it worked in Britain not surprisingly appeared as a luxury of a sort because paupers did not actually die of hunger in Britain.[52] The rumour, never confirmed, was that Irish landlords and parishes shipped their paupers to Liverpool to be kept on English taxes.[53] All these elements have contributed to the construction of myths of two types of emigration: the noble crossing to the United States and the servile journey of those who went begging for their bread in Britain, like the poor woman from Sligo in Yeats's *Kidnappers* who went to Glagsow. No wonder then, that the Irish race was seen to have survived in the United States, whereas it was thought to have disappeared in Britain. Until the beginning of the twentieth century, the Irish community in Britain was well defined, exiled in a hostile environment, and had played an important part in the Chartist movement, in the creation of the trade unions and in the birth of the Labour Party. No one uses the expression 'Irish-English', however, although there exist localised labels such as Liverpool-Irish.

The result is that only Irish-Americans can claim they are members of the 'Irish race'. In the nineteenth century, the wealthy and influential Irish-American community wielded the overwhelming power of being able to grant a label of Irishness to political leaders in the home country. De Valera during the Anglo-Irish War could spend the entire conflict collecting funds and securing political support in the United States and no one raised an eyebrow. Today, John Hume and Ian Paisley are both regular travellers to the United States, but the same efforts are not made towards the Irish in Britain.

The one exception to this rule was when the labour issues took precedence over the national question. During the 1913 strike and lock-out in Dublin, Larkin and Connolly spent considerable time and energy in Britain collecting funds and organising political support for their struggle, but there is not the faintest trace of their even asking their American brothers for support.

The collectors of nationalist and republican funds went west, the collectors of labour and socialist money headed east. So, in October and November 1913, Irish labour leaders set out for Britain. Jim Larkin travelled tirelessly the length and breadth of Britain in his 'Fiery Cross Crusade'. In his speeches, the main enemy, more than William Murphy or the British government, was the leadership of the Labour Party and the TUC, both of which he considered to be wavering, frightened by the revolutionary masses, Irish or English, bureaucrats lulled to sleep by corruption. Larkin's purpose was therefore to speak directly to 'genuine workers', who were often Irish emigrants, and unveil the masks of traitors who refused to launch a general strike in solidarity with the struggle in Dublin. (This idea, it is worth pointing out, was considered feasible in Britain, but not in Ireland, where it was never even suggested.) The violence of Larkin's rhetoric matched his political purpose: 'hypocrites' and 'traitors' were among the milder phrases he used to describe the leaders of the British labour movement. The result was predictable. The union leaders most sympathetic to Larkin had to back down, and at the British TUC's special conference on 9 December 1913, at which the only item on the agenda was the organisation of solidarity with Dublin, the first session was devoted to a motion moved by Ben Tillett, considered Larkin's leading British ally, condemning unjustified attacks on British trade unionists. The motion was carried almost unamiously.

We have a paradox here. In terms of financial and

political solidarity, the response of the British trade union movement in 1913 is without doubt one of the most important examples of international solidarity in the history of the labour movement. This was recognised by Connolly in the aftermath of the strike when he wrote:

> I say in all solmenity and seriousness that in its attitude towards Dublin the working class movement of Great Britain reached its highest point of moral grandeur – attained for a moment to a realisation of that sublime unity towards which the best in us must continually aspire.[54]

In spite of that, his overall judgment is negative: the Dublin strikers were defeated in 1913 because of the lack or weakness of solidarity on the part of the English labour movement. Connolly, after his glorification of the 'moral grandeur' of the British working class, wrote in the same article:

> We asked for more ... [than] that the working class of Britain should help us to prevent the Dublin capitalists carrying on their business without us. We asked for the isolation of the capitalists of Dublin and for answer the leaders of the British labour movement proceeded calmly to isolate the working class of Dublin.

The reason for this condemnation is obviously not just a question of character. Connolly was a much more sober personality than Larkin and found the latter's volatile character difficult to work with, but he also asked for sympathy strikes in Britain (though not in Ireland), for British workers to refuse to handle goods that had been carried by scabs; this, in effect, was a call, albeit step-by-step, for a general strike. As this particular form of solidarity did not materialise, the reason given for the defeat in Dublin was the failure of the British working class. This interpretation of the movement has entered the historiography of the strike and become an accepted fact. For Morton and Tate, in their history of the British labour movement, ordinary British workers showed great solidarity, but the leaders did not share the generosity of their grass-roots members.[55] For Peter Berresford Ellis, trade union leaders refused to alleviate the sufferings of the Dublin workers. His conclusion is that the struggle was lost because trade unionists in England, Scotland and Wales refused to support Dubliners with sympathy strikes. In 1913, he adds, workers throughout the British Isles were at a crossroads and had to choose between reform and revolution; the Irish chose revolution, the English, Scots and Welsh chose reform.[56] For Desmond Greaves, the Dublin workers asked for action and received charity; financial help became a substitute for solidarity.[57] As for the deputations sent by the British TUC to help the people of Dublin, Andrew Boyd explains that these were not gestures of solidarity but voyages made in the hope of healing the conflict so as to remove a bad example.[58] All those analyses focus on one single point: Dublin workers lost their battle in 1913 as a result of the lack, or weakness of English solidarity. The internal weaknesses of the movement, its isolation from the rest of Ireland and the growing hostility it caused are not taken into account by these widely accepted historical analyses. In fact, most of the financial help received by the strikers came from Britain. In her research into the strike and lock-out, Anita Pincot could not find any trace of significant financial solidarity on the part of Irish trade unionists. The majority of Irish unions did not organise sympathy action, and the conflict was entirely led by the Dublin Trades Council, with the Irish Trades Union Congress playing practically no role. The workers at Murphy's *Independent* rejected a call for a sympathy strike by 629 votes to 228,[59] while the electricians at the Dublin power station refused to cut the power to tram lines.[60] From Belfast, £65 was sent to the British TUC. There was no trace of help from the Belfast Trades Council. It is clear that the leaders of the Dublin strike were far more demanding of their English than their Irish comrades.

The only explanation for this placing of the blame on inadequate solidarity from England is to be found in the national question. As long as the labour and socialist movement was geared towards the national demand for independence, all other demands were determined by the latter. The nationalist view was that English imperialism had occupied Ireland and the English people had to assume responsibility for the past by assisting the Dublin strikers. The truth of the matter, however, is summed up by Roy Foster: 'The lock-out of 1913 essentially failed for the usual reason: a surplus of non-union labour, and the inability of Dublin workers to bring any vital industry to a halt.'[61] So, English workers were called on to bear the heaviest burden because of their country's past. As they could not or would not do so, they bear the blame for the defeat of the strike in the eyes of its Irish leaders and some historians.

The 1880s were not the same in Britain and in Ireland. In Britain, the decade was marked by the growth of the New Unionism symbolised by Tom Mann, Will Thorne and Jim Larkin. In Ireland, however, the 1880s were the period of Home Rule, land agitation, the growing power of the Irish Parliamentary Party and the alliance with Liberals against the Conservative Unionists. The same turmoil assumed different forms. Tom Mann toured Ireland to recruit members for his general union, but his campaign was a failure. On his first visit to Belfast, Will Thorne wore a green scarf on which was sewn the badge of the Municipal Employees' Union. He was very nearly lynched by Protestant workers.[62] Jim Larkin created his Irish Transport and General Workers' Union in 1909 after having been expelled from Sexton's British-based National Union of Dock Labourers in 1908, a clear break with England. The attraction of nationalist Dublin proved irresistible. Both Larkin and Connolly agitated in Belfast with some success, and the great Belfast strike of 1907 and the unionisation of dockers and women in the textile industry were no minor feats, but both men eventually withdrew to Dublin because their continued influence in Belfast would have been possible only at the cost of relinquishing their nationalist commitment. Only in Dublin could they find the fervour created by the encounter of a strong labour movement and nationalism. Larkin and Connolly were nationalist militants as much as trade unionists, and Dublin was the only place where the heat of nationalism and working-class rebellion could merge. This is the only possible explanation for Larkin's and Connolly's counter-productive onslaught on organised labour in Britain.

The working-class movement in Britain could not uphold the national revolution in Ireland, since the Irish people were themselves divided on the issue. The exposure of their so-called treason in 1913 thus played a double role. It justified the break with British trade unionism and also provided a patriotic label for Irish trade union leaders under pressure from nationalists and accused of being English agents. The fierce denunciation of the 'reformist' and 'imperialist' English labour leaders should therefore be seen as much as an aspect of the anti-English campaign as a radical critique of trade union reformism.

The prevailing pattern of nationalism imposed itself. As we have seen, Irish nationalism excelled in the myth of inner purity and external corruption. Bad ideas, whether pornography or socialism, could only come from the world outside, which generally meant England. Economic difficulties were always seen as due to English imperialism, never to internal weaknesses. The decline of Gaelic was the result of an English plot, never a refusal by the Irish people to speak their native language. The leaders of the Irish labour movement shared this culture, and the reasons for defeat could only be sought outside Ireland. The Irish working class was pure, its fighting and revolutionary spirit was undaunted. It was betrayed, as the United Irishmen and the Fenians had been. There was no reflection on the lack of solidarity in Ireland itself, in Dublin as well as in the North, or on the religious and cultural reasons for the failure. Such a reflection would have necessitated a painful analysis of Irish society and of the shortcomings of the dominant nationalist tradition.

In his classic history of British trade unionism, Pelling calls the Dublin strike of 1913 the most important event of the year and attributes its character to the influence of syndicalism, which he saw as coming to Ireland from the United States.[63] It is quite clear that the new syndicalism had much in common in Ireland and in Britain. The Belfast strikes in 1907 led by Larkin were not dissimilar to those in Liverpool in 1911 under Tom Mann's leadership. Kenneth Brown, however, adds that the reasons for the unrest which caused a general sense of foreboding and a feeling that an era was coming to an end were cultural as well as social, and his point of view provides a useful indication of the difficulties and misunderstandings between the Irish and the English during the struggle in Dublin in 1913.[64] Not only were there strikes, but the traditional tenets of the family and sexual mores were under attack in the works of Havelock Ellis, books like H.G. Wells's *Socialism and the Family* and plays by Ibsen, Shaw and Wilde. Traditional morals were also seen as being sapped by the suffragette movement which generated adverse reaction as much for its denial of the domestic role of women as 'moral guardians' as for any other reason.

If the social and ideological turmoil was general, the landscape in Britain and Ireland was not the same. In Ireland, family and religious values were still strongly adhered to. Connolly's dispute with De Leon is, as we have seen, a good indication of the strength of those values. Women might have been suffragettes in Britain, but in Ireland their militancy was mostly turned into nationalism in the south and Unionism in the North. Constance Markievicz in Britain would have been a suffragette leader. Larkin was at the same time a dangerous socialist for the nationalists and a dangerous rebel for Dublin Castle. An example of this cultural rift was seen in the financial solidarity campaign in 1913. The

British TUC provided a significant share of the help to the locked-out workers in the form of food shipments acquired and shipped through the co-operative movement. The leaders of the British labour movement were very proud of this achievement which they saw as proof of the strength and efficiency of co-ops, and sent messages of congratulations to the co-operative movement. In Ireland, the nationalists, of whom the most virulent was Arthur Griffith, said that the money should have been given directly to the strikers to be spent in Dublin shops and that the shipping of food was nothing less than an English plot to reduce Dublin shopkeepers to bankruptcy. The deadlock was complete. The other major example of this cultural rift was the sad affair of the campaign to 'Save the Kiddies'. Mrs Montefiore was, it must be remembered, an English feminist. It must also be remembered that the reaction of Connolly and Larkin to the campaign against Mrs Montefiore was most cautious, and they tried their best to avoid a head-on clash with the Catholic hierarchy over the issue. Although the church's campaign against the 'kidnapping' of Irish children proved to be a fundamental turning-point in the conflict, it is still not seen today as the major cause for the defeat of the strike. John Newsinger is not untypical in claiming that the British labour movement's refusal to take sympathy action was much more important than the hostility of the Catholic church.[65]

James Larkin left Dublin after 1913 for the United States where he was politically active and later imprisoned for two years for making seditious speeches. Reprieved in January 1923, he went back to Ireland in April and his journey home was a triumphant return. Thousands of American workers bid him farewell at the docks; in Southampton, thousands of English workers came and paid tribute. In Dublin, the streets were packed with a welcoming crowd. His car was hauled through the city by young men. No fewer than five orchestras played nationalist tunes and the demonstrators were shouting the old slogans of 1913 strike. By 1923, however, Larkin

had become a Communist and was not quite in keeping
with the mood of post-war Irish society, and his influence
was due as much to nostalgia as sympathy for his
newly-espoused Bolshevism.

But Connolly and Larkin both have their monuments
in Dublin, even if they did not achieve their revolution.
They have both been inserted into the collective memory
and imaginary history of the Irish Catholic and
nationalist people. This naturalisation has been achieved
through a series of breaks from whatever is 'not Irish',
achieved through symbolic gestures. The highest such
gesture is, of course, the sacrifice of one's life for one's
country, and in this respect Connolly's naturalisation is
more successful than Larkin's. But even in the case of the
revolutionary and Bolshevik Larkin, his flamboyant
tactics, his refusal to compromise and his sense of the
spectacular allow him to be placed in the camp of
uncompromising nationalists opposed to the treachery of
the constitutionalists.

For the demands of labour to be accepted as a natural
element in Irish politics, the labour movement had to
break with revolutionary views about fundamental
religious and moral values, the family, sex and women's
position in society. In much the same way the Ulster
socialist William Walker was able to exert an influence
on affairs in Belfast only in so far as he did not challenge
Protestant and Unionist culture in the North. In
accomodating itself to dominant values in this way, the
labour movement became integrated in its respective
societies, North and South but, in so doing remained a
strong force for the protection of its members, although it
thereby relinquished any wider influence.

It is surprising, therefore, that for more than half a
century after his death, James Connolly has been lauded
as a 'Marxist theoretician of major importance' in spite of
this historical failure.[66] For Bernard Ransom, Connolly,
against the background of an ossified Marxism which
had become crude and determinist, is seen as reintegrat-
ing into historical materialism the values of the Catholic

religion and of Gaelic Ireland. He started with the central idea that 'the cause of freedom in a subject nation could not advance any faster than that of its most subject class'. But how could the working class come to power in a country where the national question occupied the entire political stage? The economic justification for socialism which predominated in the British labour movement did not greatly help him in his task. On the contrary, it contributed to the conception of Ireland as a 'backward' country whose economic development, as well as the development of 'class consciousness', needed to be stimulated by constant assistance from the experienced elder brother. In 'naturalising' Marxism, James Connolly radically transformed the question of economic backwardness. The survival of clans, of collective ownership of the land, were not signs of backwardness but premonitory signs of the socialist future. The patriot was not to regret these aspects of the past, but, on the contrary, to admire 'the sagacity of his Celtic forefathers, who foreshadowed in the democratic organisation of the Irish clan the more perfect organisation of the free society of the future'.

James Connolly was also brought in to combat the persistent propaganda of the Catholic church against socialist ideas. As we have seen in his controversy with DeLeon, Connolly, in contrast with his contemporaries in the European socialist movement, did not oppose this propaganda with materialist ideas. Instead, he attempted to demonstrate that socialism did not exclude Catholicism, since he considered the former to be a doctrine of tolerance and of respect for the faith of others. Above all, he showed that the teachings of the church could bring Catholics to agitate for socialism, on the basis of the fundamental doctrines of their church and not only on the basis of their social position. He contrasted Catholic morality, which condemned entrepreneurial values, with a Protestant morality favourable to capitalism. A return to the sources of Christianity, he argued, would show that the Catholic church could not dream up a better Caesar than a socialist society.

The political reasons for pursuing such lines of argument are very clear, but it is most peculiar that they should be presented as theoretical work of major importance. In order to enrich Marxism, was it sufficient simply to add traditional moral and national values like pieces of mosaic? Connolly wished to contest the political leadership of the nationalist struggle and did so by taking from the middle class those values which were the foundation of revolutionary romanticism, in other words the strongest ideological weapons with which the middle class secured its hegemony over the rest of the population. The very fact that Connolly's life as a political activist should have culminated in the creation of the Irish Citizen Army indicates an unsurmounted theoretical difficulty. Instead of drawing up the balance sheet of the great confrontation between the classes which constituted the 1913 strike, Connolly moved to a military domain, which is precisely where class confrontations were most confused. Perhaps no other outcome was possible, but let nobody pretend that any other outcome was sought.

We know that the founders of Marxism contributed to this theoretical backwardness. Their position rested on an absolute certainty: the primacy of class over every other historical category. For Marx and Engels, the nation was only a transitory category which corresponded to the necessities of the development of capitalism, and they predicted that the nation would begin to fade away with the development of capitalism and disappear with the coming to power of the proletariat. The national question was not provided with a statute of autonomy by Marx and Engels, and was marginalised in relation to the questions which they considered as central. When Marx and Engels were writing, England was the centre of capitalism, the dominant power in the world market, the only country where the 'objective' conditions of revolution had developed to a certain degree of maturity, and therefore the most important country from the point of view of the world revolution; Ireland only entered into

their reflections in the context of this central preoccupation. If they wrote a great deal about Ireland, it is
only because the Irish question was an important
element in English history. The broad outline of the
evolution of their thought on the Irish question is
well-known. Until the 1860s, they considered that the
English revolution would liberate Ireland from the
English yoke, but later reversed this proposition and
came to believe that only Irish independence would allow
the full development of the English working class.

This under-valuation of the national question has to be
seen in its historical context. In nineteenth-century
Europe, the national question tended to take precedence
over all other relations and the emergent labour
movement had its own specific needs. For nineteenth-
century socialists, national unity was not a goal in its
own right, but, rather, a tool which would allow the
working class to focus on its own interest. What is more,
at the very moment when Connolly's thought was
developing,

> The formation of the great national states was achieved,
> their unity was accomplished, and nationalism became
> the dominant ideology of the right; it was perceived as the
> principal danger for socialism which sought to find
> antidotes, with the aid of the International, in inter-
> nationalism.[67]

This means that Connolly's search not only took place on
hostile terrain but also flew in the face of the theoretical
preoccupations which prevailed in the rest of the
European labour movement. James Connolly was not so
much a 'Marxist theoretician of major importance' as a
classic example of the limits confronted by Marxism
when it has to deal with the national question. History is
not simply the history of class struggle, and Connolly was
an actor in a drama whose motor was not that
fundamental conflict. For all that he tried to cobble
together Irish history in such a way as to infuse it with
elements of class struggle, he was finally engulfed by

national realities and after 1916 the labour movement found itself marginalised, if not paralysed, as a result.

Notes

1   Tom Garvin, *Nationalist Revolutionaries in Ireland*, Oxford 1987, p. 23.

2   Claude Grignon and Jean-Claude Passeron, *Le Savant et le Populaire, Misérablisme et Populisme en Sociologie et Littérature*, Paris 1989.

3   Dermot Keogh, 'William Martin Murphy and the Origins of the 1913 Lock-Out', *Saothar* No. 4, 1978.

4   James Stephens, 'Come Off That Fence!', *Irish Worker*, 13 December 1913.

5   W.P. Ryan, *The Irish Labour Movement, From the Twenties to Our Own Day*, Dublin 1919, p. 225.

6   James Connolly, 'Labour in Dublin', *Irish Review*, October 1913.

7   *Irish Worker*, 8 November 1913.

8   Anne Marreco, *The Rebel Countess, The Life and Times of Countess Markievicz*, London 1969, p. 162.

9   *Irish Worker*, 29 September, 2 and 11 October 1913.

10   Stephen Walsh, 'Food and the Hungry School-Children', *Irish Review*, October 1913.

11   T.M. Kettle, 'The Agony of Dublin', *Irish Review*, November 1913.

12   *Irish Times*, 1 November 1913.

13   Ibid., 8 October 1913.

14   Ibid., 14 October 1913.

15   Ibid., 13 November 1913.

16   James Connolly, 'Labour in Dublin', loc. cit.

17   *Irish Worker*, 13 December 1913.

18   Padric Colum, 'The Dublin Public and the Dublin Employers', *Irish Worker*, 15 November 1913.

19   T.M. Kettle, 'The Agony of Dublin', loc. cit.

20   Dermot Keogh, 'William Martin Murphy and the Origins of the 1913 Lock-Out', loc. cit.

21   T.M. Kettle, 'The Agony of Dublin', loc. cit.

22   AE (G.W. Russell), *Irish Times*, 7 October 1913.

23   *Irish Times*, 1 October 1913.

24   Justin Dempsey, 'The Revolt of the Middle Class', *Irish Review*, December 1913.

25   James Stephens, reviewing Connolly's *Labour in Irish History*, *Irish Review*, March 1911.

26   James Stephens, 'Come Off That Fence!', loc. cit.

27   AE (G.W. Russell), *The Dublin Strike*, Dublin n.d.

28   Madame Markievicz, 'In Jail', *Irish Worker*, 1 November 1913.

29   AE (G.W. Russell), *Irish Times*, 13 November 1913.

30   Maud Gonne, *Irish Worker*, 1 November 1913.

31   *Irish Times*, 14 October 1913.

32   W.B. Yeats, 'On Reading Much of the Correspondence Against the Art Gallery', *Irish Times*, 8 September 1913.

33   *Irish Worker*, 2 August 1913.

34   Ernest Boyd, 'Dogmatism in Irish Life', *Irish Review*, July 1913.

35   Francis Sheehy Skeffington, *Irish Review*, June 1912.

36   AE (G.W. Russell), *The Dublin Strike*.

37   'The New Evangel', *Freeman's Journal*, 4 November 1913.

38   *Irish Times*, 21 October 1913.

39   *Irish Times*, 3 November 1913.

40   *Freeman's Journal*, 4 November 1913.

41   *Catholic Bulletin*, January 1913.

42   Michael Pheelan, 'A Gaelicised or a Socialised Ireland – Which? Socialism and Social Reform', *Catholic Bulletin*, November 1913.

43   *Freeman's Journal*, 3 November 1913.

44   Ibid., 4 November 1913.

45   Desmond Ryan, *Remembering Sion*, London 1934.

46   Michael Davitt, *The Fall of Feudalism in Ireland or the Story of the Land League Revolution*, New York 1904, p. 414.

47   *The Connolly DeLeon Controversy on Wages, Marriage and the Church*.

48   C. Reeve and A.B. Reeve, *James Connolly and the United States*, Atlantic Highlands 1978.

49   Ibid., p. 34.

50   Ibid., p. 186.

51   Robert E. Kennedy Jr, *The Irish: Emigration, Marriage and Fertility*, Berkeley 1973.

52   Helen Burke, *The People and the Poor Law in Nineteenth Century Ireland*, Littlehampton 1987.

53   Frank Neal, 'Liverpoool, the Irish Steamship Companies and the Famine', *Immigrants and Minorities*, March 1986.

54   *Forward*, 9 February 1914.

55   A.L. Morton and G.W. Tate, *History of the English Labour Movement*, London 1956.

56   Peter Berresford Ellis, *A History of the Irish Working Class*, London 1985, p. 202.

57   C. Desmond Greaves, *The Irish Transport and General Workers' Union, The Formative Years: 1909–1923*, Dublin 1982, p. 104.

58   Andrew Boyd, *The Rise of the Irish Trade Unions*, London 1985.

59   Anita Pincot, *James Larkin et ses Relations avec le Mouvement Ouvrier Britannique Durant la Grève de 1913 à Dublin*, unpublished PhD thesis, University of Paris VIII, 1989.

60   Greaves, op. cit., p. 96.

61   R.F. Foster, *Modern Ireland, 1600–1972*, London 1988, p. 438.

62   Robert McElborough, *The Autobiography of a Belfast Working Man*, typescript in Public Record Office Northern Ireland, n.d., 770/1.

63   Henry Pelling, *A History of British Trade Unionism*, Harmondsworth 1979, p. 138.

64   Kenneth Brown, 'Larkin and the Strikes of 1913: Their Place in British History', *Saothar* No. 9, 1983.

65   John Newsinger, 'As Catholic as the Pope – James Connolly and the Roman Catholic Church in Ireland', *Saothar* No. 11, 1986.

66   B. Ransom, *Connolly's Marxism*, London 1980.
67   G. Haupt, M. Lowy and C. Weill, *Les Marxistes et la Question Nationale*, Paris 1974, p. 33.

5   Intellectuals and Violence

All efforts to render politics aesthetic culminate in one
thing: war. War and war alone can set a goal for mass
movements on the largest scale while respecting the
traditional property system.

Walter Benjamin

Cultural Nationalism

We have already examined the relationship between
cultural nationalism and armed violence, as expressed by
the Young Ireland and Fenian movements, their use of
arms in poetry and their poetry in arms. The link was
further reinforced by the literary revival, Pearse's
writings before the 1916 Rising and the armed struggle
of the Anglo-Irish War. Through cultural nationalism an
Irish tradition of violence was constructed. By making
clear the nature of that construction, there is no better
way than showing the essential foreignness of this
allegedly Irish tradition.

Each country has its own brand of nationalism. In the
'open' definition of the nation a citizen is someone who
willingly shares the values on which the nation was
founded, while the 'closed' definition is based on an
essentialist view of the nation. The former includes, the
latter excludes. There was a short period during the
French Revolution when any foreigner who shared the
philosophy of the revolution was considered to be a
French citizen. Tom Paine was a deputy and Wolfe Tone
a general in the French army. By the same token, a
French aristocrat hostile to the ideas of freedom and

equality could become a foreigner, and sometimes through exile, actually became one. The French people 'grants asylum to foreigners banished from their country for the cause of the liberty. It refused it to tyrants,' declared article 120 of the 1793 Constitution.[1] In Ireland, John Mitchel could defend slavery in the United States, Fenian leaders fight colonial wars in the French Foreign Legion, James Stephens flirt with socialist ideas in France, but they were all members of the 'Irish race', as were Connolly and Larkin. In the same way, anyone born of a Jewish mother, anywhere in the world, can be buried in Israel.

In the old Soviet Union, citizenship meant sharing the fundamental values of the state: socialism, recognition of 'the leading role of the Communist party' and so on. A citizen who did not share those values might become a foreigner. The way in which writers and scientists could be expelled from their country and become foreigners, deprived of their Soviet passport, was quite astonishing but nevertheless, understandable: born in Russia, Armenia or Estonia, people would remain forever Russian, Armenian or Estonian, whatever they did, but they could be thrown out of the country and deprived of their Soviet citizenship, since being Soviet essentially meant adhering to a political and ideological system. The Soviet example serves as a reminder that a non-theological definition of the nation is not in itself a guarantee of freedom for its citizens. Each system has its own drawbacks. In the cultural definition, essentialism has it that citizens cannot lose their birthright, whatever they do, so voluntary exiles like Joyce would try all their lives, unsuccessfully, to lose their Irish identity. A laicised, or non-religious Jew, no matter how hard he or she tries, cannot avoid his or her right to be buried in Israeli soil. This can be quite irritating.

In the Irish case, what came to predominate was a cultural nationalism founded on the European, essentially German tradition. The nation is a person, composed of similar Irishmen, a race apart from others.

Its most striking feature, the language, was used as a proof of the long-standing existence of this race apart, and did not have any other practical purpose. In the case of Basque nationalism, the same process is also very clear: the language was re-invented in the 1880s and immediately became the proof of the existence of a Basque race.[2] The existence of Gaelic revealed an idyllic ancient society free and uncorrupted by foreign invasions. With the conquest by Britain came the supreme fight to reconquer the body of the nation-person, its territory, and its soul, the nation's language, culture and religion. It is the fight of the periphery against the centre, of country against town, of the genuine against the cosmopolitan, of natural virtues against modern decadence.[3]

The more the definition of the nation is of a religious and mystical nature, the more it requires the sacrifice of martyrs in a founding act of violence. For the nation to exist, its citizens must be ready to make the supreme sacrifice.

Nineteenth-century European nationalism produced a specific type of nationalism, romantic or cultural, based on land, language, race and a common past. Cultural nationalism considers the people as an organic whole and the nation as a person. Nationalism then becomes the search for national roots, the fundamental tenets of an eternal whole, its language and myths, which are not considered as shameful superstitions but as the highest expression of the national mind. Cultural nationalism is generally mixed with populism: the hidden treasure is buried in the people because the people form the oldest and thus least adulterated layer of the country, whereas the 'upper', more recent layers, have been corrupted by foreign influences and cosmopolitanism. Everything that comes from the people and from the soil is highly valued: the language, full of colour and poetry, its music, which is seen as always spontaneous and original, and its folk wisdom expressed through various sayings and tales.

For Isaiah Berlin, the first form of cultural nationalism

was German romantic nationalism, which started with the conquest and the domination of the country by France and the French Revolution. The reaction of the German-speaking people to the domination of the nation of universal philosophy and of reason thus took the form of the glorification of the individual against the collective, of the national and the historical against the universal and the 'timeless' or a-historical. During Napoleon's domination Europe, the conquered society reacted by stirring up

> real or imaginary triumphs and glories of the past, or enviable attributes of its own national or cultural character. Those who cannot boast of great political military or economic achievements, seek comfort and strength in the notion of the free and creative life of the spirit within them, uncorrupted by the vices of power and sophistication.[4]

It is no wonder that in such circumstances political life becomes a work of art and the aesthetic model is applied to politics, so that 'the political leader is a sublime artist who shapes men according to his creative design'.[5]

Young Ireland clearly bore a resemblance to such romantic nationalism. Its ideology was that of spiritual rebirth through nationhood, the history of the nation shared by a racial community struggling against foreign domination.[6] These ideas originated with the German writer Herder, though according to Roy Foster they reached Ireland through the intermediary of Carlyle.[7]

For Herder, everything proceeded according to a divine plan, including the history of humankind. Herder's history, steeped in cosmic optimism, shows that God's plan has been achieved and that humankind is everywhere what it could only be, and nothing but what it could be. Language, for example, is necessarily what it can be, where it can be, an idea that would later be taken up by Fichte. For the first time, the founding idea of modern nationalism, that political unity and national unity must be congruent, was clearly expressed: a kingdom composed of one nation is like a family, a well-kept household, while an empire with a hundred nations is like a monster deprived of life.

Although Herder's ideas were universalist and ecumenical, in the sense that he saw each race as organised according to the system best suited to its natural surroundings so there is no place for disparaging accusations of savagery or backwardness, there is nevertheless a hierarchy in the history of humanity. The difference is not racial but geographical, and in the history of humankind there is a gradual development towards advance and progress: Greece and Rome, of course, and then the northern people, whom Herder calls the Welsh, in Great Britain, Ireland and Gaul, characterised by the survival of their native language. The cream of the cream, it comes as no surprise, is the German nation, where men are tall, strong, perfectly proportioned and endowed with a warlike spirit. It is in the German nation, thanks to its primitive virtues, that Christianity returned to the simplicity of its origins with the Reformation.

With Herder, for the first time, the nation became a person, a natural entity where culture (the language), the state and territory must coincide. Fichte borrowed the idea of cultural supremacy from Herder, and with his *Addresses to the German Nation* (1808), effectively founded modern nationalism as it would be transmitted throughout Europe, and particularly Ireland in the second half of the nineteenth century, with its two main components, culture and virility.[8] Fichte explicitly spoke to men, young men ready to shed their lives for their fatherland. Men are better able to understand lofty ideals because they are permanently preoccupied with the improvement of the race. In late Victorian Britain, 'fallen women', unmarried mothers or prostitutes, were considered as potential polluters of the race, while men were the defenders of the racial purity.[9] The link between cultural patriotism and virility was a recurring theme in Fichte. It was up to young men to be preoccupied with a 'better race', and men only could 'poeticise their lives through the quest for a lofty ideal'. The preface confirms this idea: Queen Louise, the soul of the coalition against Napoleon, had only a woman's instinct, violent and obscure. Fichte translated this obscure feeling into 'ideas of men for men'.

The masculinity of cultural nationalism is a point that has not yet been sufficiently explored. Jacques le Rider has noted that one of the key elements of German nationalism, especially in its fascist and pre-fascist forms, was a strong anti-feminism which revealed a crisis of men's sexual identity.[10] Jews were in fact placed on the feminine side of society in the Nazi world-view. Patrick Pearse also insisted on a 'virile nationalism', no doubt because of his own crisis of sexual identity, while Yeats was attracted to the virility of fascism for the same reasons: 'There are moments when hatred [of England] poisons my life and I accuse myself of effeminacy because I have not given it adequate expression.'[11]

Fichte's main ideas are recalled here simply to show that the main myths of Irish nationalism were not unique to Ireland but came from foreign shores. This reminder is necessary because the themes of cultural nationalism are so repeatedly presented as distinctively Irish that it is refreshing to explore their intellectual archaeology. Reading Fichte, one finds the main lines of the argument and the whole structure of Irish nationalist thought, rather like a Viking fort unearthed in Central Dublin.

For Fichte, the basis of national weakness is individual selfishness. During the Roman conquest, some Germans were ready to accept bribes and by doing so became 'non-Germans and half Romans', effectively slaves. 'West Britons' would be the name given to their equivalents in Ireland. Thus it is that the moneyed, middle and cultivated classes have weakened the race by their maniac imitation of anything foreign. For the nation to be reborn, one must face the seriousness of the harm done like 'a virile man'.

What should the national response consist of? First of

all, national characteristics should be revered and there must be a refusal to dilute German nationality with foreign characteristics. Such a refusal is first and foremost a question of culture, so the education of the whole nation is the principal way of reviving it. The will must be educated first, the will to substitute love of place for material selfishness, whose satisfaction depends entirely on the conqueror. 'It is necessary to endeavour to improve men not on the surface, but in their most intimate thoughts: they, and they themselves, thus improved, can ensure the survival of the nation.'

The German male is the only person able to receive such an education, because the German people have clung to the household of their ancestors through their language. Others have emigrated, or adopted a foreign tongue. Only in Germany has the ancient solidarity survived. It is not a question of climate, nor of race: what is significant is the language, the main characteristic of the race. Language is not man speaking, it is nature speaking through man. Frontiers are not material but spiritual and determined solely by the strength of the human spirit.

Most interesting in relation to the role of intellectuals in the national renaissance is the part attributed to poetry by Fichte. Poetry is the second main element in a people's intellectual culture. Anybody who is able to enlarge the potential power of imagination through language is a poet, and any thinker who achieves this is also called a poet. Even though language and poetry cannot be a substitute for political independence, the writer has an important role to play in influencing public life, 'shaping it according to his views'. These are words which could have been written by Yeats. The writer can influence those who are the main actors in public life, in so far as he writes and thinks in the language of those who govern. The 'noblest principle and the most sacred function of the writer is to gather the nation and to discuss with it the most important matters'.

The proof of the nation is patriotism, that is to say the

love of a people for their country. This is not a lukewarm affair, but a passion. The leaders of a nation are not those who love with a peaceful tenderness its laws and constitution but whose patriotism is 'like a burning devouring flame, who sees in the nation the warden of eternal life and would readily sacrifice their lives for her'. Pearse's blazing patriotism, a religion that required its martyrs was nothing new.

For Fichte such readiness for self-sacrifice is the sign of a genuine patriotism:

> Such men, and all those who in the history of mankind shared the same sentiments, were victorious because the Eternal gave them enthusiasm, and such enthusiasm always gets the better over those who do not possess it. Victory belongs not to brute and muscular force, or the odds of arms, but to strength of character. Whoever sets a limitation on the extent of sacrifice, ceases all resistance as soon as the limit is reached.

The Sword and the Pen

Violence has become an Irish tradition, but these words have lost their meaning through frequent repetition. Tribal wars, agrarian crimes and urban terrorism are not specifically Irish forms of violence. What is perhaps Irish is their uniquely strong concentration in a very small part of the world.

In all the human sciences – economics, history and perhaps especially in social science – academics are happy when they are read by governing princes. If only the writer could influence political leaders, make them knowledgeable and more intelligent: this is an old and widespread dream, but one that is particularly present in the history of Ireland, where the poets thought that if they could make political leaders a bit more poetic. Ireland could become a blessed place where utopias came true. The dream has gone sour, but it has not disappeared. In this context, one particular point needs to be emphasised: despite a well-known claim to the contrary, the tasks of changing and interpreting the world are not the same, and no book of political science has ever changed reality; this means, for example, that my own opinions about modern Irish politics have no special weight simply because I have written books about Irish history. It is quite sufficient if the academic or writer provides food for thought. In that sense, whatever one's stand on armed violence, one must resist its criminalisation. Criminalisation of armed violence aims at withdrawing any legitimacy, whether historical or political, through cancelling any link, apparent or real, with history and politics.

When studying the relation between armed violence and intellectuals, we refer to armed movements which, whether one likes it or not, possess a certain amount of legitimacy and are sufficiently well established to avoid degenerating into armed groups devoid of any political perspective. When armed groups lose all legitimacy, there remains only a problem of law and order: how are they to be arrested and neutralised? But if the legitimacy lingers on, then the existence and activity of men of arms pose a serious question that is primarily political because political violence is always perceived as a major threat as it tends to monopolise all the violence of a society and identify that society as 'violent'.[12] This is the case in Northern Ireland, where the number of casualties is less than in many other places, but where political violence has absorbed all other political and social tensions. People in the North will say that the foreign media are to blame for this situation, that journalists and television crews always stir up trouble. But the Ulster press, never the last to complain about foreign coverage of local news, always runs banner headlines the day after a vicious shooting or a bombing that confirms the political power of the bomb. The use of arms in politics gives greater influence and power than the exercise of constitutional rights.

Let us avoid psychological explanations. Violence in Ireland has a history; it is not part of the Irish 'character'. None of the various forms of violence seen in Ireland is a mystery springing forth from the unfathomable depths of the Celtic soul. Conquerors invade the country, bringing with them modern civilisation; they teach rationality and enlightenment with gun and sword, and then they claim surprise when they are not always and everywhere greeted with songs of welcome. They become indignant at the ingratitude of the natives. There is nothing particularly Irish about that. The war that led to the creation of the Irish nation state had far fewer casualties than many other wars of national liberation. Moreover, it is worth remembering that peasant revolts can usefully be compared to other forms of peasant struggle in other countries.[13] Violence appears when there are no other means of expressing demands or of protesting. It arises when it is the only message that can be communicated and understood by the masters. The peasant wears himself out, he tills the land, harvests the corn, milks the cows, raises the cattle and pays the rent for land that he does not own. When the rent becomes intolerably high, how can he make his voice heard, what means does he have at his disposal? He does not know his landlord, who in many cases lives far away, quite possibly over the sea in Britain. They do not attend the same church, nor even speak the same language. There is no intermediary between the farmer and the landlord, no point of contact, no forum for discussion.

When despair is total, when the very existence of the family is at stake, farmers form groups by night, blacken their faces, maim cattle, set fire to haystacks, even kill landlords or their agents. When the number of such incidents reaches a certain level, the message is understood, the rent is reduced, evictions are deferred and a new equilibrium is achieved. Michael Davitt, the organiser of the Land League, impressed upon those who condemned the peasant outrages that when physical violence is the only means of making oneself heard, then its manifestations must be taken as messages. When Lord Leitrim was murdered in 1878,

Every tenant in Ulster knew and felt that it was by acts of this kind that the oppression of landlordism was kept within bounds and the homes of peasantry were rendered more or less secure against the fate of eviction. This is why the persons who killed Lord Leitrim and his guards were not discovered or punished by the law.[14]

There is no point in condemning violence in the name of morality, no point in denouncing it from the pulpit. As long as the message is not heard, the violence will continue. The only way of curtailing peasant outrages was to organise the farmers politically so as to make peaceful action more effective. These peasant forms of resistance have influenced other forms of struggle, including modern urban ones. Irish emigration to Great Britain, the United States and Australia reproduced there both the experience of mass political struggle learnt with O'Connell, and also the methods associated with agrarian struggles and secret societies: the destruction of buildings and attacks on the person. This was especially so when the frontiers of the industrial ghetto were clear-cut and when other forms of organisation and struggle were proscribed. As E.P. Thompson wrote in his classic history of the working class in England,

The rapid movement of men with blackened faces at night, the robbery of arms, the houghing of horses and cattle – these were methods in which many Irishmen had served an apprenticeship.[15]

These violent clashes gradually disappeared in Great Britain and France, absorbed in an economic and political system capable of channelling social tensions into discussion and compromise. Parliamentary democracy created the space necessary for the development of middle-class interests, and the other social forces were absorbed in the same space. Secret societies were replaced by open organisations, trade unions and political parties. Ireland, both in the Republic and in the North, now has a parliamentary system complete with regular elections, political parties and all the other trappings of parliamentary democracy. How then can it be a territory where paramilitaries continue to secure enough support from the people they claim to protect to keep going as they do? How come it contradicts the apparently logical rule outlined by Che Guevara, who knew a thing or two about guerrilla warfare and had no qualms about resorting to it:

> Whenever a government has achieved power through a process of popular consultation, fraudulent or otherwise, and maintains the slightest appearance of constitutional legality, the buds of guerrilla war cannot blossom.

Ireland as a whole continues to be identified with the 'tradition' of physical violence. How are we to account for the persistence of this tradition? The reasons are related partly to history and partly to contemporary political and social conditions. Resorting to violence proves difficult, if not impossible, when it is not considered a legitimate tradition. The combatants must have the feeling that they are not breaking new ground, but simply continuing what has always existed. On the other hand, it is not enough for *only* tradition and cultural models to be to hand, they need be related one way or another to actual social experience. Tribal forms of organisation in Ireland are not only a thing of the past.

Legitimisation by History

In Ireland as elsewhere, political violence appears as a social regulator when the traditional state mechanisms are not available. Until the early twentieth century, the bulk of the Irish population did not possess a government, a police force, a system of justice and a state apparatus which was legitimised by being representative. This only came about with independence.

The existence of an armed movement within a modern society is always a sign of the state's failure to have its authority recognised. The armed movement develops in the vacuum where state authority is absent. The state existed in nineteenth-century Ireland, but as a set of institutions alien to the majority of Irish people. In such conditions, minor demands as well as major ones were negotiated in the shadow of political violence. Daniel O'Connell in his campaign for Catholic emancipation and then for Repeal was opposed to armed risings, but, as we have seen, his vocabulary was warlike and in his negotiations with the British government he always used the threat of armed rebellion if he was refused a hearing. Parnell acted in much the same way in his dealings with London: he was the best protection against anarchy, Fenianism, Ribbonism and all the other dark forces that were ready to set Irish estates ablaze. In February 1881, Michael Davitt was arrested. Parnell protested but refused to leave Parliament to lead the rent strike. He went to Paris instead, where he met Victor Hugo, and the British press denounced him as a dangerous revolutionary, which is exactly what he wished – to be seen as a rebel without actually taking part in any violence.

Little has changed in the intervening century. In the North moderate nationalists secure support for their politics by using the threat of a war much worse than the present one, while Unionist leaders tried to obtain the repeal of the Anglo-Irish agreement by using the same line of argument: they might be pushed aside by more sinister leaders.

It is therefore difficult to draw a firm line between the constitutionalist and the 'physical force' traditions in Irish nationalism. The two traditions support one another. This means that in Ireland armed violence has acquired historical legitimacy through the use made of the threat of violence by its declared opponents.

The way in which the national myths were constituted has also played a considerable role in the legitimisation of armed violence. This is where cultural nationalism is an essential link. The more the definition of the nation is racial (the nation as a person, constituted by people of the same race, culture, religion and language), the more

it excludes others and thus militarises political life,
which tends to become the protection of the community's
cultural borders. The more the definition of the nation is
religious and mystical, the more the founding act of
violence and the sacrifice of martyrs are deemed
necessary. For the nation to be born, or born again, its
citizens must sacrifice their lives for it. The nation need
martyrs, its pound of flesh. All political tendencies,
constitutionalist as well as 'physical force', churches and
cultural associations, endlessly celebrate the cult of the
martyrs considered to be the real founders of the Irish
nation. This applies most particularly, of course, to the
vanquished heroes because their defeat and their
youthful deaths ensured an uncorrupted and untainted
reputation. They were never rewarded with privileges or
honours, and posterity can therefore transmit their total
lack of self-interest and their total devotion to the cause.
Wolfe Tone, the Fenian leaders and, closer in time, Bobby
Sands have all been defeated in their rebellion, but today
they have their statues or tombs in front of which
prominent personages come every year to deliver a
speech and keep a reverent silence. Constitutionalists
like O'Connell, Parnell and Redmond, however, do not
rouse such commemorative passion. What such continuity makes clear for today's combatants is that their
predecessors' fight has always been vindicated by history
and that there is no reason why their present fight
should not in its turn be vindicated, that once again
republican heroes should not be granted pride of place in
the next round of history textbooks. History plays a part
in the present violence because any social movement
looks to the past for models.

The second set of explanations lies with territorial
politics. When others are a threat, it becomes important to
avoid them and to create a territory where one feels
completely at home, surrounded by friends and neighbours who can be trusted. When the process of avoidance
and inclusion becomes this important, it spreads
throughout the body politic. The majority needs it

because it feels threatened by those against whom it discriminates, while the minority needs it because it is the only way of securing some of the advantages which the more powerful keep to themselves. John Darby has shown how the marking out and defence of territory leads 'spontaneously' to the militarisation of politics in which relations are always those of victory or defeat, gain or loss of territory. This can lead to a policy of 'ethnic purity' then justified by history, 'race', religion, language. We are back to cultural nationalism and to the part played by intellectuals as they reinforce or erode the border.

As armed violence was closely linked to cultural nationalism, intellectuals, poets and journalists played a great part in its legitimising process. It is worth nothing that although ever since the current round of 'Troubles' began in Northern Ireland, no 'great names' have been found supporting or even vaguely sympathising with paramilitaries of either camp, this does not mean that silence is enough. Writers and other intellectuals have supported non-democratic forms of political intervention, and primarily physical violence; their words sent out men to shoot and to be shot. In a period of accelerated social and political change, they felt they were being crushed by modern civilisation and were attracted by what Ernst Bloch called 'anti-capitalist romanticism'. One way of asserting themselves was through clinging to an imaginary past and its traditional values, all the more precious as they were crumbling and thus rapidly becoming elitist values. Nostalgia for the past can find some pleasure in archaic forms of struggle.

The gunman or the bomb-maker, an artist of sorts, will find day-to-day activities exceedingly monotonous. Analogous to the contempt of the soldier for civilian life is the contempt of the poet for daily drudgery, for a society which he feels does not respect him. From time to time, these two images coincide, are incarnated in the one person. The Easter Rising was the perfect example of heroic death seen as a work of art by the poets who sacrificed their lives at that time.

The poet, just like the warrior, is a prophet whose cry seeks to awaken the 'slumbering masses'. He takes up his pen as the warrior takes up his sword, and for the same reason: because he thinks that all other means of intervention have been exhausted. Ever since Thomas Davis, the pen and the sword have been the two traditional arms of the Irish people.

At the very best, when it is overwhelmingly approved of, armed violence is a transfer of political power. At worst it is a confiscation of political power which replaces participation in the political process by the mass of the people. John Sullivan recalls in his history of Basque radicalism how as a 'gesture of solidarity' an ETA commando kidnapped the boss of a firm whose workers were on strike. The strike stopped immediately. There could be no better example of what is meant by the 'confiscation' of political power by an armed group. In the same way, the poet who bestows upon himself the status of a prophet wishes to 'awaken the people'. To be understood or approved is not really his aim, he simply wants to be heard. The principle is the same today; modern methods of communication have only served to accelerate the same process. The bomb, the kidnapping, the latest book, the latest political statement or the latest record must be seen and heard on the six o'clock news. There is nothing surprising about the way in which the combatant, who can grab the attention of the multitude with limited means and in the shortest space of time, grips the fascination of the poet. The flashing brilliance of words, the brilliant flash of bombs, the spectacular escape, the successful attack, the capture of a train or the explosion of a car-bomb are the Booker Prize-winners of armed violence. There are bloody echoes to the poetic thunder and the bombs produce literary rumblings.

Let us be clear. In the case of contemporary Northern Ireland, we are speaking of war, not riots, angry demonstrations or 'spontaneous' clashes with the police. Northern Ireland is the site of organised killings. The tensions due to the withdrawal of politics into ethnic frontiers are to be found elsewhere, not least in the United States, Great Britain and France. In those countries, so far, there is no war, civil or otherwise, there are no permanently organised groups of paramilitaries. What makes the difference is not the number of casualties. More people died in Los Angeles in a few days in 1992 than in almost six months in Northern Ireland, but Los Angeles is not 'at war' in the way Ulster is. For a state of war to exist, armed violence has to become the key point of political life as it has in Northern Ireland. It has become the focus of a society's politics and engulfs all other tensions.

This simple point is not realised in those European countries where there is diffuse sympathy for the Republicans because they seem to be fighting on behalf of an oppressed community. I read regularly in the French press that violence in Northern Ireland is created by unemployment, poverty and bad housing. But rioting has nothing to do with war: it is a sign of social rebellion, anger or despair. In recent years there have been riots in Britain and France, in Brixton, Toxteth, les Minguettes, Vaux-en-Velin and Newcastle, but these have not developed into 'war' as those in Belfast and Derry in the late 1960s did. The Fenians were quite right from their point of view in their refusal to mix nationalism with specific social demands. Agrarian agitation and social unrest generally stop at the brink of open warfare. People will die for ethnic or tribal values, not for the programmes of political parties.

How can one confuse war and rioting? When a group of youngsters smashes windows and loots shops, this can be called social delinquency, but not war. War is a situation in which well organised groups of people, generally men, trained in the use of guns and explosives, prepare a spectacular coup, sometimes for months or even years. It has nothing to do with a fit of anger. It might as well be claimed that the IRA unit in Gibraltar was wiped out because British society was angry at IRA outrages. It seems to me a fraud to mix the two. But for the media, it is an unquestionable fact that unemployment, poverty and armed violence are always related. Violence in Northern Ireland is attributed to the economic situation. The Haagerup Report at the European Assembly was drafted with the specific object of seeing whether European Community funds could alleviate the conditions in which violence thrived. If poverty is the yardstick by which a society's susceptibility to political violence is to be measured, then most of Europe, let alone the rest of the world, should be constantly torn apart by warring groups. The difference is that in Northern Ireland there really is a war, and that, even without paramilitaries, politics would be militarised. In Paris whenever a bus or a train driver or conductor is attacked, the network on which the incident has occurred immediately comes to a halt. The efficiency or otherwise of this reaction is irrelevant: what it means, fundamentally, is a principled rejection of physical violence. There are virtually no strikes against armed violence in Belfast, because people do not go on strike against the casualties of war. In other words, because of a war situation, the tolerance, the degree acceptance of this particular type of violence is very high, whereas the degree of 'acceptance' of most other forms of social delinquency is very low in Belfast compared to other European cities.

Social unrest is not about borders, and the answers are social and political. Wars are about borders, that is to say lines, real or perceived, that have been culturally constructed, including those drawn by intellectuals. Collectively, Irish intellectuals have played a great part in the construction of that border. It is not enough for them simply to deny their support for the men of violence: they have now to contribute to the destruction of cultural borders as their contribution to peace.

Anything that destroys the tribal border is by definition conducive to the process of peace. This intellectual work is urgent because social and political figures very seldom undertake the job. This pessimistic view is based on the observation of those different actors and their refusal to admit any blame laid at their doors. 'I' am always right and 'they' are always wrong. London has been able to stand by Northern Ireland, a part of the United Kingdom where a person can get or be denied a job or a house on account of his or her religion. For half a century, successive British governments allowed this state of affairs to continue in Northern Ireland. Did anyone hear a word of regret? London became interested, along with the rest of the world, with the riots of 1968. Then, for a long time, the London government treated Northern Ireland as above all a criminal problem: by uprooting the paramilitaries the way to a peaceful solution would be found. So, quite logically, any attempt at weakening the tool of justice against 'criminals' was paramount to taking sides with the criminals. Enquiries into misbehaviour by the police or army become nearly impossible, thus proving the paramilitaries right on all counts. A simple idea was forgotten: whenever armed violence acquires some sort of legitimacy for a significant section of the population, it becomes a political problem. Any attempt at criminalising a political problem will increase the difficulties as the attempt itself will become part of the process of legitimisation of armed violence.

The paramilitaries cannot be wrong either. They defend their own people, are ready to die for them, and criticism of their activities coming from the enemy is to be expected; from their people, however, any criticism is seen as treachery. Very occasionally it is admitted that the bomb went off too early or too late, but on the whole the thousands of victims all died according to plan.

Ulster Unionists refuse to admit that maybe there was, or is, some discrimination against Catholics in the North. Enquiries about quotas and employment are always welcome when they take place next door. Nationalists find it hard to admit that there are strong radical traditions in the Ulster Protestantism, because those traditions are not in the nationalist mould, and so condemn all Protestants as a group of reactionary bigots.

The churches cannot be wrong. Violence is of course

condemned from the pulpit, but Ireland is still a place where civil society is essentially religious, and if the price of diminishing sectarian tension is the secularisation of society, then the price is too high. Better a few deaths every week than the genocide of unborn babies or the massacre of marriages through legalised divorce. The Catholic church therefore opposes an integrated school system and proposals for a change in the Catholic values embodied in the Republic's constitution.

The Irish government cannot be wrong, and Charles Haughey 'had no apology to offer' for the fact that Irish society stuck to its fundamental values, thus turning anybody who did not share those values into foreigners.

People and institutions – the state, political parties and the churches – are all rigid in their certainties, yet extraordinary as it may seem, every one of those institutions considers the people of Northern Ireland as narrow-minded, bigoted and archaic and advises them to be tolerant and open-minded. Institutions which seem unable to admit one iota of wrong-doing are asking 'the people' to love each other, to understand each other, to make peace. Who are those 'people', though, if not voters and church-goers? Are they being asked to take the lead, and then their leaders will follow suit?

Although it is difficult to offer specific political solutions, it is clear that evolution in society will loosen the grip of militarism on Irish society. Whatever separates politics and territoriality is a move in the right direction. War is about the control of space considered as 'homogeneous'. In that context, Article 2 and 3 of the Irish constitution, which lay claim to Northern Ireland as an integral part of the Republic's territory, have a dramatic effect because they are precisely about territory. Any advance in the process of secularisation of Irish society, North and South, is a move towards peace because it dissolves the frontiers that the paramilitaries claim to defend. Such a step was the election of Mary Robinson, which no territorial politics could claim as a victory. In the North, how can one defend Protestant territory if it becomes unrecognisable because pubs and sports centres are open on Sundays? How is a Catholic area to be recognised if condoms are change at discos and schools are integrated? In the same way, any step in Irish society that increases the status of Irish women, in terms of jobs, education or control of private life, means a loosening of the grip of militarism on Irish society as a whole.

On the question of the 'border' that enables war, gender is one concept that has not been sufficiently explored. Religion, politics, secret societies, structure of work and the high status of male jobs all underline the fact that Ireland is a very masculine society. This is related to military violence because militarism is one way of keeping the distance between men and women when the job status and political responsibilities can no longer achieve that purpose. Paramilitaries are, in their overwhelming majority, men, even if the IRA has a few women members (unlike Protestant paramilitary groups), those women must 'look like men' because women engaged in military activity are breaking important taboos, so they have to relinquish their 'womanhood'. But if they do so, they create further problems; Countess Markievicz, for example, had to fight hard to be recognised as an officer in the Citizen Army, and had to relinquish her man's uniform and wear skirts on parade. The 'culture of intimidation' is a man's culture. In Belfast, the expulsion of Catholics and of 'rotten Prods' always took place in firms which were predominantly male in their workforce, shipyards, engineering and aircraft factories, while there are no similar examples in the textile industries in which women workers form the majority. A number of authors have noted the machismo of republican paramilitaries.[16] The fact that religion assigns to men the role of bread-winner and of soldier, to women that of mothers, wives and nurses is also of great consequence. Conversely, the mixed associations crossing the borders contain a great number of women, often in their majority.

Peace People is an obvious example, a movement which has never been analysed as a feminist movement but which deserves to be, as a movement of protest against the total control of politics by men. Other inter-community organisations like Protestant and Catholic Encounter (PACE), the new wave of peace groups (Peace Train and New Consensus) are also very feminine, and composed of women and of men who 'refuse to be men' in the traditional Irish sense. It is worth noting that one of the places where regular and numerous contacts take place across the religious divide is the school, where most teachers are women, even if those contacts are regularly described as a man's affair.

In this dissolution of the border, intellectual work is important, in history, notably, but more generally speaking, in establishing non-sectarian and universal values.

Notes

1 Gérard Noiriel, *La Tyrannie du National, Le Droit d'Asile en Europe 1793-1993*, Paris 1991.

2 John Sullivan, *El Nacionalismo Vasco Radical*, Madrid 1988, p.12.

3 Seamus Deane, *Heroic Styles: The Tradition of an Idea*, Derry 1984, p.7.

4 Cited in Conor Cruise O'Brien, 'Paradise Lost', *New York Review of Books*, 25 April 1991.

5 Ibid.

6 R.F. Foster, *Modern Ireland, 1600-1972*, London 1989, p.312.

7 Ibid., p.311.

8 J.H. Fichte, *Addresses to the German Nation* (trans. R.F. Jones and G.H. Turnbull), London 1922.

9 Martine Spensky, 'Assistantes et Assistées: Les Femmes Comme Agents du Changement Social en Angleterre', *Les Cahiers de l'Observatoire*, Janvier 1991.

10 Jacques Le Rider, *Modernité Viennoise et Crises de l'Identité*, Paris 1990.

11 Cited by Conor Cruise O'Brien, loc. cit.

12 Michel Maffesoli, *Essai sur la Violence Banale et Fondatrice*, Paris 1984.

13 Eric Hobsbawm, *Bandits*, Harmondsworth 1972.

14 Michael Davitt, *The Fall of Feudalism*, New York 1904, p.137.

15 E.P. Thompson, *The Making of the English Working Class*,

Harmondsworth 1968, p.483.
16 See, for example, Frank Burton, *The Politics of Legitimacy Struggles in a Belfast Community*, London 1978, Rosita Sweetman, *On Our Knees*, London 1972, and Eileen Fairweather, Roisin McDonough and Melanie McFadyean, *Only the Rivers Run Free – Northern Ireland: The Women's War*, London 1984.

6   Dissolvers of Borders

The authors and literary works discussed so far all aimed at establishing the borders and delimiting a territory for the coming power of the urban middle class. Within less than a generation, new intellectuals began a dissolving work that aimed at clarifying the founding myths of the nation. What came to be known as revisionism in the 1960s in fact started much earlier and, when one remembers the passion involved in a war of liberation, the intellectual courage that was required for such dissolving reflexion was truly admirable. Two landmarks are worthy of further study in this respect: firstly the *Bell*, a literary, social and cultural magazine published during the war years by Sean O'Faolain and then by Peadar O'Donnell until 1954, and secondly Sean O'Casey's theatre, the power of which is still felt today.

The *Bell*

It is almost impossible to imagine the full extent of the Irish Free State's cultural isolation during what was, in the South, known as 'the emergency' and rather less euphemistically as 'the war' everywhere else in Europe. October 1940 saw the publication of the of first issue of the *Bell* dedicated to providing Ireland with a much-needed modernising and outward-looking perspective across a broad range of social and political issues.

Although it has been persuasively argued by Terence Brown that 'the emergency' was no more a period of isolation and cultural protectionism for the majority of

Irish people than the preceding years had been, the fact remains that, early in its life, the war was remarkably absent from the pages of the *Bell*, a magazine whose explicit purpose was to break down the country's cultural isolation.[1] In July 1941, a special Ulster issue opened with an editorial in which Sean O'Faolain argued that partition was not so much political as psychological, yet the magazine's readers might have been forgiven for not knowing that Ulster was at war, for nowhere in the magazine was the conflict even mentioned. The world war was written about in the *Bell* for the first time only in December 1941, more than a year after the founding of the magazine, in an editorial entitled 'Dare We Suppress that Irish Voice?', a cry for government assistance for Irish writers whose incomes had fallen catastrophically since the outbreak of war. In April 1942, a comparison was made between Ireland and the great industrial countries which placed the bombing of towns alongside slums and workhouses as the price to be paid for industrial development. The January 1943 issue saw the first unambiguous protest against the silence surrounding the war: 'One of the great omissions in this war is that our newspapers have no foreign correspondents ... This is lowering and undignified. It dwindles us. It means we are not learning by the experience of others.' In an effort to broaden the horizons of Irish readers, the July 1943 issue published a poem by Federico García Lorca and another, in French, by Louis Aragon. In September 1943 the protest against war censorship became more forceful. In an editorial entitled 'Silent Ireland', radio news broadcasts were taken to task. The Battle of Sicily had begun and Mussolini had resigned, and the Irish public was waiting anxiously for the Sunday night news. The first news item was that ten thousand people had come together for the annual Croagh Patrick pilgrimage, the second the Cork conference of Muintir Na Tire (the People of the Land, a farmers' organisation). The news from Sicily ranked third. Irish radio's sense of priorities, the *Bell* argued, was completely wrong. The same issue published another poem by Aragon, a poet who had come to symbolise French resistance to the Nazis.

In January 1944, the editorial dealt with the question of Irish neutrality, defending the policy against British and American criticism. Neutrality, it argued, was a declaration of independence, but the price to be paid was silence. The great issues of the time, above all the competing ideologies of Communism and Nazism, were not discussed in Ireland, and it was feared that this silence threatened the quality of the nation's intellectual life. Finally, in February 1944, an explicit link was made between the war and modern Irish history in an editorial which compared the guerrilla campaign being waged by Tito's partisans in Yugoslavia with the Anglo-Irish War of 1919.

The *Bell*'s attitude to the war was, therefore, that neutrality had increased Ireland's cultural isolation, but that other countries should not draw the conclusion that neutrality was not a legitimate option and that the efforts needed to limit the resulting damage were the responsibility of the Irish people rather than the international community.

The *Bell*'s Cultural Policy

The *Bell*'s editors chose the magazine's name precisely because it had no historical roots, no echo in Irish culture. The old symbols were as dead as Brian Boru, killed by the victory of their bearers and new symbols had to be created.[2] In its third issue, readers begged the journal to adopt a more militant tone. Collectively, the editorial board claimed that ancient controversies were deadlocked. The magazine was young, just as the nation was young: neither could be constructed on the basis of old shibboleths; the *Bell*, therefore, would be devoted to facts, but this did not mean a return to empiricism. Ireland's nineteenth-century struggles were conditioned by two great systems of thought – nationalism and

religion – which had now become two great mysti-
fications. The *Bell* was conscious of the blank left in
people's minds and wanted to fill it with modern and
simple ideas, above all by abandoning the legacy of
hatred left by the Civil War and protecting and extending
democracy. In other words, the intellectuals associated
with the magazine wanted to create a secular society and
the *Bell* can be seen as a modernising force in a country
paralysed by the glitter of the past and hypnotised by the
gleam of the future. Ireland had to face reality and rid
itself of its obsession with the glorious past and
imaginary future. The main obstacle to the modernisation of Ireland was the idea of a national culture
based on linguistic homogeneity, and the *Bell* argued
that the Gaelic League and the modernisation of
industry made strange bed-fellows.[3] The rift with the
past sometimes led to bitterly ironic conclusions – Sean
O'Faolain's article on the 25th anniversary of the Easter
Rising, for example, glorified the Civil War as the best
thing that could have happened to the Irish people
because it had roused them from their romantic dreams.

Looking in bookshop windows, O'Faolain saw few book
by Irish writers, while work by the country's greatest
contemporary authors, Joyce and O'Casey, was censored
and banned. The Dail tried to ram Gaelic down young
children's throats, but all its discussion of the language
issue was conducted in English. The country was
dominated by hypocritical humbug, by a middle class
swollen with religion, profits and ignorance, leaving it
devoid of hope or inspiration.[4] Celtic revivalism and
religion had stifled literary life and led to a formidable
censorship system, the aim of which was to leave people
in ignorance. For how long, the *Bell* asked in June 1942,
had its readers not read or heard an open, public and
frank discussion of birth control, freemasonry, unmarried mothers, divorce, homosexuality, venereal disease or
prostitution? Ireland was cut off from the rest of the
world, its leaders were frightened because the world was
so close, hammering at the nation's gate. 'The world is

wicked. we are good. The world will contaminate us. We must keep out of the world,' the nation's rulers seemed to be saying.[5]

Exile, however, was not seen by the magazine as providing a solution:

> We who remain in Ireland and sometimes grow bitter and warped and silent – are we, also, a lost generation? And those of us who unwisely go … are they, also, of a lost generation? … Can you jump off your own shadow?[6]

The *Bell* had a political line, even though it was often muted or concealed. Ireland was a young country and the ashes of a dead mythology stifled all generous and creative projects. Through patient and persevering intellectual work, the Irish people had to bring a dead culture back to life, but in Ireland intellectual work was difficult and intellectuals were constantly insulted:

> 'pseudo-intellectuals', literary cliques, hackneyed journalists, or even worse, were being treated as harmless maniacs. Which is the worst situation for a political prisoner, and in that sense, all intellectuals in Ireland could be considered as political prisoners.[7]

For the *Bell*, political and artistic truth could not be confused with the views of the nationalist and Catholic majority of the population. The journal would show that Ireland was more varied than it looked, and the editors' aim was to reveal this variety by publishing literary work by Frank O'Connor, Flann O'Brien, Eric Cross, Brendan Behan, Elizabeth Mercier, Michael Farrell and others. Another of the *Bell*'s chosen tactics for revealing the full variety of Irish life and culture was to denounce Celtophilia, censorship and ignorance of the North, all of which it saw as stifling Irish culture.

Celtophilia

What had happened to the enthusiasm of the Gaelic League's early members? Those who had shared the excitement of the early days of the struggle for the

revival of the national language would scarcely have
believed possible what was happening half a century
later with the disappearance of all colour and inspiration
from the language movement. The deterioration of early
Gaelic revivalism was, the *Bell* believed, appalling, and
teachers wrote in despair at the way the language was
being taught.[8] When University College Dublin
appointed W.J. Williams as professor of education, the
Gaelic League organised demonstrations against his
appointment because he was not sufficiently fluent in the
national language.[9] The Gaelic Athletic Association
called for the resignation of the Minister for Defence
because soldiers were allowed to play Anglo-Saxon sports
like hockey and soccer. With a war raging in the world
outside, such views struck the *Bell* as complete
madness.[10] The younger generations brought up since
independence had lost all sense of history because, as
taught in Irish schools, history had become sham
Celtophilia. Irish was the official language, yet the Gaelic
League kept up an endless stream of complaints. The
enemy was no longer seen as Britain but the Irish state
and its civil servants, the church and Anglo-Irish writers,
especially Yeats and O'Casey. Anglo-Irish writing was
denounced as a colonial literature fit to be read only by
the English and West Britons. The cinema was in the
hands of Jews, those eternal enemies of Christianity.
Europe was in ruins, but for Celtophiles this was a divine
blessing as the old continent would turn to Ireland as her
guide and example when the war was over and the Irish
would once again redeem the world and help to
re-establish Christian values.[11]

Under the appropriately ironic title 'Twenty Years
A-Withering', Naosc A'Ghleanna gave three main reasons
for the difficulties confronting Gaelic. Enthusiasm for the
language had been broken by the Civil War, while
compulsory teaching of Gaelic had created a hatred of the
subject by pupils and parents alike. Finally, the anointed
wardens of the Gaelic temple were spiteful personalities;
the nation's leading cultural institutions – the Gaelic

League, the Gaelic Athletic Association, the Catholic Truth Society and the Irish Academy of Letters – had all been engulfed by the bourgeois tide, and he characterised the Irish revolution as a middle-class 'putsch'.[12] Naosc A'Ghleanna's sardonic proposals for the revival of Gaelic were even more devastating than his criticisms. He suggested publishing a Gaelic newspaper with horse-racing news, making Gaelic compulsory in all official functions, publishing in Gaelic all books banned by the censor and, finally, if all other measures failed, making it a crime to speak Gaelic. Overnight, the Irish people's militancy would be brought back to life.

The *Bell* Against Censorship

How would the future judge the history of censorship in Ireland without blaming the narrow-mindedness of Irish nationalists? The *Bell* waged a constant war against censorship and directed a harsh spotlight on what it termed 'the stupidity of Irish patriots'. Principled opposition to censorship was ever present, both in the magazine's editorials and in its literary and cultural criticism. Flann O'Brien wrote a stinging attack on 1935 Act regulating opening hours and the control of dance-halls, while Joyce's death provided Henry Bellew with an opportunity to write a piece on 'Censorship, Law and Conscience', and there were also articles on Senate debates on censorship and numerous editorials on the subject.

The most fascinating piece on the subject of censorship is, however, a long interview with Doctor Hayes, a member of the censorship board and the official film censor. A doctor, hero of the Easter Rising and historian of Franco-Irish relations, he watched two films a day, a load made heavier because, in addition to the usual moral censorship, the Emergency Powers Order brought censorship of war films. The commission banned Charlie Chaplin's *The Great Dictator* as gross propaganda from beginning to end which was likely to cause riots and bloodshed. Censorship, according to Doctor Hayes, should operate on a very simple moral code: there are principles on which civilisation and family life are grounded, and anything which insulted or threatened those principles was to be banned. Scenes of 'lascivious' dances were cut from films. *Gone with the Wind* was banned because the cuts suggested by the commission were not acceptable to the film's distributors. Two of the most important taboos were, of course, divorce and abortion, and distributors who wished their films to be shown in Ireland had to be extremely careful to suppress any frivolous depiction of the holy state of matrimony. When a film script included a divorce, the criterion according to which the board decided was a simple one: did the film show divorce in a positive or negative light? If a divorced wife was shown to end up leading a wretched existence, the film might be passed, but nothing which depicted happy or contented divorcees could be shown in the Free State. Occasionally, Doctor Hayes almost allowed aesthetic and other considerations to get the better of him; watching a French film, he was appalled by the adultery and other ungodly activity it depicted, but the actors all played their parts so well that he claimed it almost broke his heart to ban the film from Irish screens.

Throughout, the *Bell* waged a relentless campaign to prove that 'moral principles' were nothing but a smokescreen concealing a desire to muzzle intellectual and creative life, stifle all public debate and inhibit the exchange of ideas. Such objectives had nothing to do with the church, morality or Christianity. The debate about Kate O'Brien's *Without My Cloak* was very clear in this respect. A Catholic journal in Britain had greeted the book as a notable contribution to Catholic literature, while an Irish magazine had replied that a novel which dealt with the most attractive features of sexual sin could not be deemed a Catholic book: Catholic literature had to be of the sort that could be read aloud in the family. The *Bell* responded that such attitudes had nothing to do with literature or the beliefs of the Catholic church, but were directly inspired by puritanism, which was, of course, an English rather than an Irish system of belief. After all, was it not puritanical Victorians at Trinity College who had denounced the bawdiness of Gaelic literature?[14]

Censorship, the *Bell* argued, was not moral but political, and aimed at protecting Ireland from all foreign influences. It was the climax of a patriotism gone berserk. Bishop Lyons exposed the dangers of the radio and the cinema: young people ran the risk of absorbing ideas hostile to their national culture. For Daniel Corkery, the only patriotic artists were painters, not writers, because only they had really cut the link with Britain. For Senator Kehoe, in a debate on censorship, 'famous writers' were famous from an international point of view, according to criteria alien to Irish culture. The effect of such views on intellectual life was disastrous. Anyone who wanted to succeed in Ireland had to pay tribute to Catholicism and nationalism. The most pernicious effect was that writers ended up practising self-censorship if they wished to have their work published.[15]

The *Bell* and Ulster

The amount of space devoted to Ulster in the *Bell* was impressive for a Dublin-based magazine of limited resources. Two numbers of the magazine were given over to special issues on the North, one in 1941, the other in 1942, both of them published in July to coincide with the most important date in the Ulster calendar. Belfast Protestants, Orange spokesmen, Unionists church leaders and others were all given a voice in the *Bell*, and there were numerous articles by Ulster authors in addition to the two special issues.[16]

If one bears in mind the magazine's avowed objective, which was to present Ireland in all its diversity rather than as a homogeneous Gaelic-speaking, Catholic nation,

the reasons for Ulster's central role in the *Bell*'s editorial
project are obvious. People living in the North were
called Irish, and yet in their majority they did not share
the manners, the morals, the religion or the politics of
their Southern brethren, and neither did they accept the
essential pillars of Irishness as defined in the Free State
– nationalism and Catholicism. The dominant values
stifled political and cultural life in the South, and the
magazine believed that one of the best ways of lifting the
lid was to write about Irish people who did not share
those values but nevertheless lived in an area claimed by
its constitution to be part of the Southern state.

So the *Bell* set about explaining Ulster to Southern
readers, who were advised to stop sniggering at Northern
Protestants, even though their case was often so poorly
presented by their Unionist leaders, whom it called the
chief 'whiners of Europe'. Peadar O'Donnell and Thomas
Carnduff insisted on the working-class origins of
Orangeism, showing that it was sometimes in the name
of their 'Orange values' that Belfast's workers had
rebelled and organised in trade unions. The second angle
of attack was more obvious: the *Bell* presented Northern
Protestants' fears about the South in a sympathetic way.
When Northern Protestants objected to the priest-ridden
nature of Southern Ireland, what sensible person could
disagree, the magazine asked. When a Northern
Protestant complained that he had previously enjoyed an
Irish jig, but now, as soon as a fox-trot was heard, the
Gaelic Leaguers immediately withdrew in protest, the
result was that Protestants in their turn refused to dance
to traditional Gaelic tunes. In a more obviously political
vein, Sean O'Faolain wrote that partition had been a
catastrophe above all for the South, as it served to
reinforce the country's homogeneity and defensiveness
against the outside world. He claimed that the
manuscripts he received from Dublin were self-centred
and lacking poetry and humour, whereas those sent from
Belfast revealed that the six counties were related to a
vast empire, and through it to the world, so that

Northerners were truly 'twentieth-century Irishmen'. Peadar O'Donnell was even more vehement: Dublin was a dead and paralysed city and the only true capital of Ireland was Belfast, which had to speak out for the whole country as it was the only city that was closely connected with the rest of the world.

The *Bell*'s contributors sometimes overstated their case about Southern fear of the Protestant North, of course, as if the six-county state was devoid of sectarianism and discrimination and any such fear was simply of progressive modernisation. The denunciation of the South as a backward country, dominated by the Catholic church, was part and parcel of their own shibboleths. But what mattered was that the North came to play a not unimportant part in the *Bell*'s attempt to modernise intellectual life in Ireland. Making the invisible visible is an important task for intellectuals, which is why the pages of the *Bell* are well worth re-reading before entering into contemporary debates on modernism and post-nationalist Ireland. Because the *Bell*'s writers were creative intellectuals who had no wish to replace old cultural fetters with new, self-imposed ones, their vigour and buoyancy make the magazine relevant reading to this day. The *Bell*'s writers and editors were great dissolvers of borders.

Sean O'Casey

Sean O'Casey was not a famous playwright at the time of the great events which led to Irish independence – the 1913 strike and lock-out, the Easter Rising, the Anglo-Irish War and then the Civil War. He spent that crucial period studying the world around him and educating himself. He practised the Irish language at Gaelic League meetings, read Shakespeare and intervened in the great debates of those trying times, testing his way with words in polemical articles. Should socialism come before nationalism? Should Ireland follow the British model of economic development or try to shape its Gaelic soul? Then came his famous quarrel with Countess Markievicz on the direction taken by the Irish Citizen Army, whose mission it seemed to him was to defend the workers and not their fatherland. This insolent young man was condemned and then expelled from Connolly's militia. Sullen and surly, he did not take part in the Easter Rising. In his history of the Irish Citizen Army, O'Casey clearly does not agree with James Connolly's decision to hand over a working-class force to the cause of middle-class nationalism. Later, he would not fight in the war against the British. Desmond Greaves, among others, would conclude that O'Casey's critical views of Irish nationalism were founded on this withdrawal and that they act as a continuous self-justification for his political cowardice.[17] Time has, however, finally begun to heal these wounds, and it should now be clear that it was a great blessing for Irish literature that Sean O'Casey was rebuffed by Connolly and Countess Markievicz. Had O'Casey fought with the Irish Citizen Army and died in 1916, or later at the hands at the Black and Tans, there would have been no Dublin trilogy, no Joxer, no Fluther, no Jack and Nora. From a literary point of view, it is much better that Patrick Pearse is now in the mausoleum of martyrs and that O'Casey lived to write the plays which are still performed on stages across the world.

Having been shoved aside by history, or, perhaps, having removed himself from the historical stage, O'Casey reinvented Irish history from above and from below. From above because his most famous plays, the Dublin trilogy, deal with the great founding events of the nation: *The Plough and the Stars* with the insurrection in Dublin, *The Shadow of a Gunman* with the Anglo-Irish War and *Juno and the Paycock* with the Civil War. The national question is, of course, central in these events, which nevertheless take place in the background, beyond the tenements in which the plays are set. The social movements and conflicts dearer to O'Casey's heart appear much later, for example in *Red Roses for Me*, which took as its theme the great strike and lock-out of 1913. It was as if the writer had first to settle accounts with the national question and then break away from it.

O'Casey can be said to have reinvented history from below because he chose to depict the key turning points in Irish history from the point of view not of the famous but of ordinary people, the poor and those living on the margins, women from the Dublin tenements. The guns are still smoking and the corpses are hardly buried, but the war is over and the task now is to create a new body politic built on a contradiction: political power draws its historical legitimacy from the gun, but must bring an end to the rule of the gun. Such dreadful events, such emotional agony, can only be resolved in mythology, in the endless celebration of heroic fantasy. In reality, of course, the veterans are offered pensions, nursing care, government jobs and commemorative speeches and medals. That was the non-lyrical stage when political poems coalesced into pompous prose and crystallised the deepest religious and social conservatism, precisely the time when O'Casey should not have blown up metaphorical monuments or punctured tricoloured balloons. The destruction of nationalist shibboleths was, of course, particularly abhorrent to those who used them as political trinkets. O'Casey adopted a posture of exile, initially partial or 'internal' and later complete or 'external', and therein lay the basic difference between the rioting against Yeats and Synge and that against O'Casey. Yeats wanted to be recognised as a leader of the nation, and in Ireland during the literary revival there was a brief period when such writers could think that they were or, or might become, the people's Moses. In his theatre, by contrast, O'Casey clearly stated that he was no messiah, no fili, no high priest of nationalism. 'I am not one of you,' he seemed to be saying, 'I am packing my bags and leaving this island.' The insult went deep.

In order to make his journey both simpler and irreversible, O'Casey dissolved the border, and it is obvious that the great dissolvent of traditional values is that which abolishes the cult of armed violence. In his *Autobiographies* (written in the third rather than the first person), O'Casey states on a number of occasions that he had no military vocation: 'He was no soldier, never would be, he felt it ... Sean was no warrior. A harper maybe, playing others into battle. But no warrior himself.'[18] Some of his early writing, however, shows that O'Casey was perfectly capable of writing in a very martial spirit, and his history of the Irish Citizen Army contains literary rumblings that could easily have matched any bellicose speech. In 1913, 'Discontent ha[d] lighted a blazing camp-fire in Dublin,' and the coming fight would be 'The Irish Armageddon between Capital and Labour' (the capitals are O'Casey's own). The new Irish Citizen Army 'would make their resisting power irresistible, a power that would quickly change their disorganised ... units into a huge immovable unbreakable Roman phalanx'. Jim Larkin's speech announcing the event was reported with glee: 'It would be a long and bitter fight between the Titans of Capital and the Titans of Labour,' and the workers had to learn organisation and discipline so their physical force could be turned into an effective army.[19] Whatever denials he might make later in life, these passages show that O'Casey could on occasion be just as militaristic as Countess Markievicz or his other opponents.

The break with violence is clearly indicated as a break with nationalism. O'Casey objects to the change which took place in Connolly whereby 'the high creed of Irish Nationalism became his daily Rosary'.[20] If Connolly retained his following despite his new nationalist position, this, O'Casey argued, was because 'of the under-developed comprehension by the workers of the deep meaning of the labour movement ... The call of the National Tribe appealed to them more strongly than the call of the Tribe of Labour.'[21] When the tricolour was hoisted on Liberty Hall it was greeted with an immense ovation, and O'Casey's bitter comment was, 'A novel pageant ... is always a sweet luxury to the uneducated Irish nature.'[22]

This early experience began to forge in O'Casey's mind what would later become a theory about armed violence. His characters, and above all the women in his plays, are the very opposite of his old foe in the Irish Citizen Army, Countess Markievicz, who thought she would go straight to heaven if she died for Ireland, talked of 'the joy of looking along a gun at the heart of an English soldier'[23] and wrote of the Easter Rising:

> The memory of Easter Week with its heroic dead is sacred to us who survived. Many of us could almost wish that we had died in the moment of ecstasy when, with the tricolour over our heads, we went out and proclaimed the Irish Republic, and with guns in our hands tried to establish it.[24]

Armed struggle as such is the way in which labour is swept up by nationalism and absorbed by 'the national tribe'. As soon as a military unit is formed, what matters is training and discipline, parades and target practice, while ideas and politics take second place. The conclusion is obvious. If the objective is to create good soldiers, traditional nationalist organisations are much better training schools than trade unions or the old-fashioned political parties of the left. The military parade is an occasion when 'the infantry swinging along at a quick march' show 'the civilians the way to walk'.[25] For O'Casey, the participation of the Irish Citizen Army in the Easter Rising was a catastrophe: 'Nationalism gained a great deal and lost a little by its union with labour in the insurrection of Easter ... Labour has lost much and achieved something.'[26] When the workers turn to militarism the red star turns green and the infantry shows civilians how to march. In O'Casey's anti-heroic fantasies, however, it is clear that he believed civilians are at their best when they show soldiers how to walk.

This idea will never desert him when political violence appears in his drama. The plays where war is present, the Dublin trilogy and *The Silver Tassie*, are a demilitarisation of the epic. War is systematically presented from the point of view of civilians – mainly women – who try, unsuccessfully, to teach the soldiers how to walk. The characters in his plays are generally working-class or poor, and the intrusion of war into their lives does not represent a dramatic break with reality, just a brutal worsening of conditions. In their working lives, they sell their labour-power, their physical strength, their time, for a price called wages. In the same way, when they have a rifle in hand they become cannon fodder for a price that is set by agreement. To those who want to present war as a sport for adults, O'Casey retorts that it is not a game, that heroic speeches are paid for with maimings that are traumatic for all concerned, but particularly for those for whom physical strength is the only commodity they have to sell on the market.

The Silver Tassie is a particularly good case in point. The scene in the second Act could be a workshop in a big factory. The soldiers do not fight but work, 'cold and wet and tired', for twelve hours a day lifting, carrying and piling up shells. Meanwhile, those who do not work – shirkers in wartime, the wealthy in peacetime – are warm and cosy: 'shells for us and piano for them'. The wives at home are expecting the weekly wages, 'the seperytion money'. When the men are tired, their wives' duty is to help revive them: the household needs the money. Even if the women's nagging is sometimes almost unbearable, it does not turn them into monsters. In the first Act, Harry Heegan, back with his friends from a football match, is in no hurry to return to the front. His mother never stops bickering at him: 'Watch your time, Harry, watch your time.' While he tells her about the highlights of the football match, she helps him dress and slips a sandwich into his pocket saying, 'You've got a few minutes to spare.' Mrs Foran begs someone to fetch her husband, who is blind drunk, to help get him back on the boat; if the men do not return to their barracks they run the risk of being charged with desertion and their women will not be able to draw the separation money – 'An' no one thinking of me and the maintenance money.' When

Harry has lost his legs, his mother can't help balancing the accounts, saying, 'He's bound to get the maximum allowance.' She shares with Mrs Grigson in *The Shadow of a Gunman* the same preoccupation with hard cash: 'Do the insurance companies pay if a man is shot after curfew?' Men go to war for the same reason that they go to the factory, not because they like it but because they must risk their lives in order to earn a living. When Teddy Foran, Harry Heegan and Barney Bagnal are all safely on board, Mrs Heegan is at last satisfied: 'Thanks be to Christ that we're after managing to get the three of them safely away.'

In the Dublin trilogy, war is obviously of a different kind. The fighters are volunteers not conscripts, but they are no more heroes than those who fought in Flanders. They are simply human beings who are killed and wounded, and O'Casey does not spare us the details of their injuries. 'Seven wounds he had – one entherin' the neck, with an exit beneath the left shoulder-blade; another in the left breast penethratin' the heart,' is Mary's description of a death in *Juno and the Paycock*. 'The bullet he got in the hip in Easter Week was bad enough; but the bomb that shattered his arm ... that put the finishin' touch on him,' is Mrs Boyle's remarkably unsentimental description of her own son Johnny's injuries. There is no triumphant music to celebrate the wounded and the dead, only blood and gore. Nora in *The Plough and the Stars* does not mince her words: 'An' in th' middle o' th' street was somethin' huddled up in a horrible tangled heap ... His face was jammed again th' stones, an' his arm was twisted round his back ... An' every twist of his body was a cry against the terrible thing that had happened to him.' In the same play Lieutenant Langon cries, 'Th' stomach is ripped out o' me; I feel it – o-o-oh, Christ! [...] me gettin' me belly ripped asundher! [...] D'ye think I'm really badly wounded, Bill? Me clothes seem to be all soakin' wet ... It's blood ... My God, it must be me own blood!' Captain Brennan tells of Jack's death: 'He was shot through th'

arm, an' through th' lung ... I could do nothin' for him –
only watch his breath comin' an' goin' in quick jerky
gasps, an' a tiny sthream o' blood thricklin' out of his
mouth, down over his lower lip.' When the legless Harry
Heegan attends a welcome-home celebration after the
war at the end of *The Silver Tassie*, he asks to be laid
face-down on the floor, 'An' I will turn over on my back,
then wriggle back again on to my belly and that's more
than a dead, dead man can do!'

Any attempt at making sacrifice heroic, at justifying
the mutilations of war, is quickly stifled by recalling the
harsh realities of life. Johnny, Juno's son, has lost an arm
during the Easter Rising and claims that he would gladly
do so again, 'for a principle's a principle'. His mother
retorts, 'Ah, you lost your best principle, me boy, when
you lost your arm; them's the only sort o' principles that's
any good to a workin' man.' In the same play, a neighbour
tries to cheer up a recently bereaved woman with the
words, 'He died a noble death,' to which the mourning
mother responds harshly, 'An' I'll go on livin' like a
pauper.'

Another way of dissolving the romanticism of war is to
show that, deep down, the so-called heroes are cowards,
afraid of war but afraid not to join in. 'I saw fear glowin'
in all their eyes,' says Nora in *The Plough and the Stars*.
Men's fear of not taking part because of pressure from
their friends is a strong theme in Nora's exposure of
military heroism. In her view, Jack has no greater desire
than to stay with her, and in the middle of the Easter
Rising she asks, 'An' he stands wherever he is because
he's brave? No, but because he's a coward, a coward, a
coward!' In this context Captain Brennan's description of
Jack's death becomes a parody of a heroic speech: 'He
took it like a man. His last whisper was to "Tell Nora to be
brave; that I'm ready to meet my God, an' that I'm proud
to die for Ireland." An' when our general heard it, he said
that "Commandant Clitheroe's end was a gleam of glory."
Mrs Clitheroe's grief will be a joy when she realises she
has had a hero for a husband.'

The fighters are no heroes, but wounded and maimed soldiers driven to war out of vainglory and cowardice, afraid of expressing their love for life. Their wives and mothers send them to the slaughterhouse for a price and then cry over their corpses, weeping over the long list of victims at wakes: 'Hasn't the whole house, nearly, been massacred? There's young Dougherty's husband with his leg off; Mrs Travers that had her son blew up be a mine … Mrs Mannin' that lost wan of her sons in an ambush … an' now poor Mrs Tancred's only child gone west with his body made a collandher of.' It is clear from this litany that the names of the victims are not soldiers with ranks but breadwinners who are all introduced by the women as husbands, sons or brothers.

Moreover, as O'Casey's soldiers are not heroes, they have no rights over other survivors of the conflict. 'We who have come through the fire unharmed must go on living,' says Susie as she drags Jessie away to the dance in *The Silver Tassie.*

Irish republicans were understandably angry at O'Casey's attacks on their fundamental beliefs, primarily in *The Plough and the Stars*. They were furious above all because the playwright had inscribed fear in the hearts of the 'heroes', turning them into cowards or pretenders, turning them, in fact, into women. In classical Freudian terminology, Nora is castrating her lover Jack when she wants to deprive him of his fighting power. O'Casey's answer to his critics was, in certain respects, trite: he resurrected the hackneyed idea according to which there can be no genuine courage without fear, and quoted George Bernard Shaw in *Arms and the Man*. To Mrs Sheehy-Skeffington, who blamed him for having turned all his male characters into cowards, he answered, 'Langon, wounded in the belly, moans for surgical aid. Does she want me to make him gather a handful of blood and murmur, "Thank God this has been shed for Ireland?" I'm sorry, but I can't do this sort of thing.'[27]

This argument would be more convincing were it not for O'Casey's later plays. When Michael is shot by a

fascist in *The Star Turns Red*, there is no whining and no
blood, just good old-fashioned heroism. He asks his friend
Jack, 'Now, my fist – close it ... Now, my arm, raise it, lift
it high ... Lift it up, lift it up in the face of these
murdering bastards – The Clenched Fist!' There is no
blood or gore either in the same play when Jack's death is
reported: 'Jack's gone west. Got it in the heart.' Red Jim's
final speech is as declamatory and heroic as the gesture
of the clenched fist: 'He fought for life, for life is all; and
death is nothing!' Ayamonn in *Red Roses for Me* glorifies
heroic death: 'When a true man dies, he is buried in th'
birth of a thousand worlds.' All the paraphernalia of
heroism is there, the death of a 'true man' and his
religious sacrifice for the rebirth of the world. Death, in
The Star Turns Red and in *Red Roses for Me* is a
transmutation as the hero dissolves himself in the great
common cause. His blood reddens the stars or the sky
above Dublin. There is no fear in the hearts of those who
fall for the sake of their class or their union – 'Our
comrade's gone, but there's no weeping ... The cause he
lov'd is in safe keeping,' goes the funeral chant in *The
Star Turns Red*. A drop of blood is like a dewdrop.
Although Sean O'Casey answered Mrs Sheehy-Skeffington, 'I can't do this sort of thing,' he would later show
that he was quite able to do precisely 'this sort of thing'.

The way in which the victims of war are presented is,
of course, a judgement on the conflict itself. There are
very few gaping wounds or wheelchairs to be seen in the
memorials erected in English towns and French villages
after the First World War. Novels, plays, poems and films
which give pride of place to mud, blood and horror rather
than military heroism are obvious expressions of pacifist
sentiment. O'Casey's best known work obviously forms
part of that literary tradition, but, as we have seen, some
of his later work glorified armed conflict of a different
kind.

In his own way O'Casey stated that the Dubliners
living in tenements had nothing to gain but wounds or
tombstones from nationalism's armed insurgency.

O'Casey, like many members of his generation, saw the solution to the world's problems in Marxism – 'There's only one war worth havin': th' war for th' economic emancipation of th' proletariat,' as the Covey declares in *The Plough and the Stars*. In nationalist conflicts, the people were always the losers in O'Casey's view. As Seumas proclaims in *The Shadow of a Gunman*, 'I draw the line when I hear the gunmen blowin' about dyin' for the people, when it's the people that are dyin' for the gunmen.'

After independence, most writing of any value or consequence in Ireland has concerned itself with the task of dissolving the border. First poets and novelists then historians started questioning society's fundamental values and revising Irish history. One of the most powerful weapons in the armoury of the defenders of the tribe was censorship, which was as much a defence of Ireland's cultural borders as a religious and moral decision. Such intellectual endeavour made the scholars' life much less pleasant for a while.

Notes

1 Terence Brown, *Ireland: A Social and Cultural History, 1922–1979*, London 1981, p.175.
2 *Bell*, October 1940.
3 Ibid., April 1941.
4 Ibid., September 1941.
5 Ibid., March 1943.
6 Ibid., May 1943.
7 Charles Kickham cited in ibid., April 1942.
8 Ibid., December 1941.
9 Ibid., April 1943.
10 Ibid., June 1943.
11 Ibid., May 1942.
12 Ibid., June 1943.
13 Ibid., October 1941.
14 Ibid., September 1941.
15 See Julia Carlson (ed.), *Banned in Ireland, Censorship and the Irish Writer*, London 1990.
16 See, for example, the August 1942, April 1943, May 1943, July 1944 and August 1944 issues of the *Bell*.

17   C. Desmond Greaves, *Sean O'Casey, Politics and Art*, London 1979.
18   Sean O'Casey, *Autobiographies*, London 1963, Vol.1 p. 368.
19   Sean O'Casey, *The Story of the Irish Citizen Army* in *Feathers From the Green Crow*, London 1962, pp. 181–4.
20   Ibid., p. 226.
21   Ibid., p. 230.
22   Ibid.
23   Constance Markievicz, *Prison Letters*, London 1987, p.xiv.
24   Ibid., p. 41.
25   Sean O'Casey, *Autobiographies*, loc. cit., p. 157.
26   Sean O'Casey, *The Story of the Irish Citizen Army*, loc. cit., p. 181.
27   Sean O'Casey, 'The Plough and the Stars, A Reply to the Critics' in Ronald Ayling (ed.), *Blasts and Benedictions*, London 1967.

Conclusion

Traditions ... are traditions only in so far as their followers have no possibilities other than to suffer them lest they be excluded from their community. Directly they are questioned, traditions appear for what they are: an expression of power relations.

Catherine Quiminal

Eric Hobsbawm writes that no definition of a nation is universally accepted since the nation is a subjective notion which cannot therefore be defined in rational terms.[1] There are countless subjective definitions of the nation, as something which people think they are attached to, or in Renan's view, something akin to a permament referendum. There are objective definitions of the nation, founded on territory, economy, culture, 'race', language, religion and so on. None of these is universally accepted.

The number of definitions is the sign of a real difficulty. Sociological research that touches on sensitive areas, like religion in Northern Ireland or ethnicity in Britain, tends to ask its questions in subjective terms like 'What religion do you think you belong to?' or 'What ethnic group do you consider yourself to be part of ?', thereby using the concepts of *perceived* religion or *perceived* community. For want of an accepted term, Hobsbawm adopts the same stance. Nationalism exists when a sufficient number of people *consider* they are members of that nation. Hobsbawm writes, 'This book assumes that any sufficiently large body of people whose members *regard themselves* as members of a nation will be treated as such.'[2]

I share with Eric Hobsbawm and Ernest Gellner the idea that the nation is not an objective reality or a sleeping beauty waiting for men of action, poets, princes or would-be martyrs to waken it. Ireland has not always been a nation. It became a nation because it was constituted by a culture, or a set of cultures, and on the basis of those cultures the will developed to make the culture and the state one and the same. For Gellner, 'The tendency of political societies is to expand their borders as far as their culture,' and the partition of Ireland can be seen as the direct application of that historical 'rule'.[3]

Modern culture in a developed society cannot transmit itself through the family or even a small-scale community. Education has become so complex that only the state is able to bear the burden, and socialised education lies at the very heart of nationalism.[4] According to this theory, nationalism is the product of modernisation and industry, and it comes as no surprise that the golden age of nationalism in Ireland was also that of the modernisation of the state and of the education system. Between 1861 and 1911, there was a ten-fold increase of those employed by the Irish civil service, from 990 to 9,821.[5] The Land Commission, the Congested Districts Board, the Department of Agriculture and Technical Instruction and the National Insurance Commission were all created between 1881 and 1911. There were new opportunities for members of previously excluded groups, Catholics, women and the lower-middle class. An intermediate system financing Catholic secondary education was set up in 1878, and the Royal University became the National University in 1909.

Cultural nationalism was first borne by historians and linguists, then by writers, playwrights and poets. They wanted to rouse the people with stories of an everlasting nation and an ancient civilisation. This mission was then taken up by journalists and other urban intellectuals, and at the rural level by teachers and shop-assistants.

For a social historian, the nation is a well defined space

containing individuals who do not know each other, but who possess, or think they possess, common interests. The consciousness of belonging to a common people can only be constructed through a national identity involving common ancestors, founding myths and symbols. Where the state already exists, it is central to the process of creation of national identity through elections, a currency, an army and a parliament. For Gellner, it is nationalism that created nations, not nations that created nationalism. This is certainly so in the case of colonised or otherwise dominated countries, but in the case of well established powers, the nation-state sometimes created nationalism. In France, for example, foreigners did not exist in the modern sense of the term until the 1870 war with Germany. Before that watershed, the notion of 'alien' existed only in the values of local communities and in abstract legal principles.[5] The centralised state, working through parliament, the popular press and the education system, managed to convince the majority of French citizens that they should share a common preoccupation with the national question, and the main national myths of Gaulish ancestors and the wisdom of the peasantry were created at this time. And, of course, along with the pious definition of the Frenchman came the new concept of the foreigner identical from the north to the south of the country, and varying only with the international situation. In every household, children acquired a common, stereotyped view of the English, Germans and Italians.

In Ireland, cultural nationalism was constructed by the poetry of the Young Irelanders, the autobiographies of the Fenians, the songs and poetry of Gaelic story-tellers, the fairy-tales written by Standish O'Grady, Douglas Hyde and W.B. Yeats, petrified by Daniel Corkery into an official history in *The Hidden Ireland* which outlined the main features of an eternally sacred nation. Daniel O'Connell and Charles Stewart Parnell perceived the nation in rationalist terms as a homogeneous collectivity of educated citizens, and also built up centralised mass political organisations. Cultural nationalism, on the other hand, tended to see the nation not as a state but as a distinctive historical community which evolved into a synthesis of the traditional and the modern, as John Hutchinson has pointed out. Such a community cannot be reconstructed from above by the state but only by the people from below.[6] So cultural nationalists, in a line descending directly from Herder and Fichte, considered themselves primarily as educators, establishing schools and universities and cultural organisations such as the Gaelic League, agricultural co-operatives, temperance leagues, the Gaelic Athletic Association and so on. Their ideas were taken up by a younger intelligentsia, barristers, solicitors, doctors, higher civil servants, teachers, clerks and shop-assistants like Michael Dempsey in *The Clanking of Chains*. The success of cultural nationalism was 'to create a counter-culture, socialising through their networks an elite, a revolutionary strike force'.[7] I hope I have been able to show in this book that cultural nationalism was an essential process in forging the identity of the Irish people in the sense that it helped to delineate culturally who was an Irish citizen and who was not. The Irish citizen was a Catholic, a Gaelic-speaker and a man. Women and Protestants were definitely not citizens, culturally speaking. The cultural nationalist phenomenon was so strong that no law was required to exclude 'aliens' from the avenues of political and cultural power.

Not surprisingly, such nationalism by definition refuses any rational definition of its tenets, historical or sociological. The religious charcter of Irish nationalism was enshrined in the orations of Patrick Pearse. A nation is a church, and a church is always founded on the blood of its early martyrs. The Old Testament of the nationalist church is found in the adventures of Cuchulain and Finn and in the Ulster cycle. The New Testament is revealed in the lives of Tone, Emmet, Pearse and Connolly, the gospels according to Saint Wolfe, Saint Robert, Saint Patrick and Saint James.

Gellner warns us that the study of the prophets of

nationalism and of the myths they created or spread will not teach us much about nationalism as an historical and sociological phenomenon, but we can learn a lot about the process of self-identification of a people, as long as we do not mistake this for historical reality. A revealing late twentieth-century example of this process is provided by the current fashion among some Celtophiles for discovering traces of feminism and primitive socialism in ancient Irish society.

Nationalism in general, and cultural nationalism in particular, permitted the shift from religious to secular politics to take place. By turning the nation into a sacred myth and nationalism into a religion, it enabled masses of people to withdraw from established churches. This displacement is not unique: it accompanied the establishment of all nation states. In the United States citizens swear allegiance to the constitution and salute the star-spangled banner, while in France people contemplate the national past in front of war memorials. The reverse of this phenomenon took place with the collapse of the Soviet Union where the religious iconography that had held Soviet citizens together shattered because it had become far too closely identified with, indeed the property of, the ruling political party. This was a serious mistake on the part of the ruling elite: war memorials and statues, heroes and saints, should be revered by all citizens, members of all political parties and of none. If they become part of the party system, the state runs the risk of crumbling with its all too transient values. Indeed, a revolution may be described as a change in the fundamental values of the state.

In Ireland, every political leader has had to go, at least once in his or her lifetime, to Bodenstown to celebrate Tone, Pearse and the Founding Fathers, and one can easily imagine why the Catholic church did not at all like this shift from the religious to the secular. The nineteenth-century mass nationalist movements were strongly identified with Catholicism. In spite of the Catholic affiliation of the new nationalism, or rather because of it, nationalism was considered as a fundamental break from religion, a secularisation of Irishness. The gods did not disappear, but they bore names of men living on earth. The conflict between cultural nationalism and the Catholic church was therefore all the more severe as it was a fundamental conflict between two faiths, two religions. The Catholic church said that only God, Christ and the saints deserved to be revered on earth. Only God deserves the sacrifice of a human life. Cultural nationalism declared that a Gaelic poem, the land and the soul of the nation were equally worth dying for. Ireland was not France, where the village teacher and the parish priest competed for local influence, because in an Irish village the teacher was employed by the church. But by rousing the same religious fervour for the Gaelic language or folk literature, the local intelligentsia forged formidable weapons for its future influence. The church quite rightly felt threatened by this secular enthusiasm which ate away at the only true faith. The question at issue was one of power.

I do not wish to become mystical in my turn by denying the importance of what I do not believe in, as if my incredulity could with the stroke of a magic wand wipe out the congregations in churches, theocratic states and warlike nationalist enthusiasms. Atheism is not a religion and does not sweep away religion as a social, political and cultural phenomenon. In the same way, national atheism, by which I mean the refusal to believe in an everlasting and sacred nation, should not drive us to a blindness in the face of cultural nationalism. Let us be irreverent and revisionist in our writing of history, but let us not be blind. Let us repeat that most national history is a fairy-tale invented for grown-up children in the nineteenth century. Let us repeat that the nation is not an essence but a social and historical construction. For there is no such thing as a 'natural' nation, any more than there are 'natural borders', a phrase which French children of my generation heard a thousand times from teachers who told us that France was a divine creation because the country had assumed the form of a harmonious hexagon peopled with Gaulish ancestors, even though these 'natural borders' have, of course, changed hundreds of times as a result of war and conquest.

In the same vein, geographical insularity is not in itself a cultural feature, although it is used in Britain to 'prove' that Britons were born a nation of sailors, the 'natural' builders of a vast empire whose rise was inevitable in an island awash with imperial genes. The same geographical feature is used in Ireland to 'prove' that Ireland was protected against foreign influences and thus remained pure and uncorrupted by invasion. When a group of political leaders claims to know their ancestors inside out, we should be wary, because this means that they have a closed definition of the nation, founded on the soil, the 'race', the language. They are the upholders of a closed, ethnic nation as opposed to the open conception of a chosen nation. Why should it be easier for someone to be a good patriot when he or she was born inside the 'natural' frontiers? Those who choose to live in France because of the country's freedom of religion and human rights have chosen to be French citizens – a positive decision which, logically, should be considered as more reliable than the accident of place of birth. Why should chosen patriotism be considered as more fragile than inherited patriotism?

Irish culture means Irish blood. A pinch of salt is enough to make fresh water undrinkable, a drop of the right blood is enough to turn a normal human being into a staunch patriot as long as he adheres strictly to the precepts of cultural nationalism. Michael Stephens's grandparents were called O'Coole, but, 'the O vanished when they came to America, so they could get through immigration faster, alphabetically'. But the 'O' remains like the smile of the Cheshire cat, when everything else has disappeared. So, on Saint Patrick's Day, they come out in their tens of thousands on Fifth Avenue in New

York, with their bishops, their schools, their policemen
and their firemen, wearing green ties and green dresses,
waving green banners, all searching for their vanished
'O'. Away from home, cultural nationalism becomes even
purer.

Ironically enough, cultural nationalism contributed
greatly to an ethnic definition of the nation whose main
drawback is not that it closes the external frontiers,
which after all, is the purpose and function of
nation-states, but also closes them on the inside, more
and more to restrict the breathing space of those who find
themselves within the frontiers. If there are 'genuine
Irishmen', for those who use such terms, the number of
genuine citizens is bound to diminish constantly.
Because a genuine Irishman will always find another
Irishman who is even more genuine, who knows his
history better or considers the other's Gaelic broken and
faulty. Those who do not share the values considered as
vital for the country are asked where they were born, as
Jim Larkin was in 1913. How, with his socialist ideas,
could he be a true-born Irishman? For Gellner the state
always tries to go as far as its founding culture permits.
This attempt is rarely successful, and historically there
are mercifully few examples of culturally homogeneous
nation states. When this does take place, as it has in the
former Yugoslavia, the world is horrified. When the same
process took place in Ireland, there was no such outcry.

Historians and other academics have done an excellent
job of trying to re-establish a secular view of the Irish
nation. Louis Cullen has recently shown, not without a
certain degree of glee, that Daniel Corkery did not really
understand the poems he was glorifying, while linguists
and Celtic researchers have shown that Markale does not
understand Gaelic and draws his information from
secondary sources. The effect of this scholarly bebunking
is however, limited: Daniel Corkery will continue to be
read and Markale will still be considered as a fine scholar
of the Celtic world. It is better to share illusions than
destroy them. We are therefore caught in a painful

contradiction: nationalism is a construction, an ideology, but it is not an illusion. Nationalism is in people's heads, so people have to be shot in the head to dislodge those wrong ideas. One person's pornography is another's eroticism. One person's chauvinism is someone else's patriotism. They are patriots, they are in love with an illusionary country and tradition, with an image, with a representation. What else can one be in love with?

Notes

1 Eric Hobsbawm, *Nations and Nationalism Since 1780, Programme, Myth, Reality*, Cambridge 1990, p.8.

2 Ibid., p.9.

3 Ernest Gellner, *Nations et Nationalisme*, Paris 1989, p.86.

4 Ibid., p.61.

5 Gérard Noiriel, *La Tyrannie du National, Le Droit d'Asile en Europe 1793-1993*, Paris 1991, p.90.

6 John Hutchinson, 'Cultural Nationalism. Elite Mobility and Nation-Building: Communitarian Politics in Modern Ireland', *British Journal of Sociology*, December 1987.

7 Ibid.

Index